MW01287541

Love Letter to Ramah

TIM AMSDEN

LOVE LETTER TO RAMAH

Living Beside New Mexico's
Trail of the Ancients

University of New Mexico Press | Albuquerque

ISBN 978-0-8263-6658-0 (paper)
ISBN 978-0-8263-6659-7 (ePub)

Library of Congress Control Number: 2024939561

Portions of two chapters of this book were published in different versions in *New Mexico Magazine*. Chapter 11, "Bluebird Flour," appeared in the September 2004 edition, and chapter 30, "Bear Heart," appeared in the August 2005 edition.

A portion of chapter 31, "Sundance," was published in a different version in *The Bear Is My Father: Indigenous Wisdom of a Muscogee Creek Caretaker of Sacred Ways*, Marcellus "Bear Heart" Williams and Reginah WaterSpirit, Synergetic Press, 2021.

A portion of chapter 17, "Medicine Wheel and a Blessing," was published in a different version in *Female Nomad and Friends: Tales of Breaking Free and Breaking Bread Around the World*, Rita Goldman Gelman, Three Rivers Press, 2010.

Cover image by Nancy Dobbs
Designed by Felicia Cedillos
Composed in Chaparral Pro

*This book is dedicated to my love and co-creator, Lucia Amsden;
to the memories of my son, Adam Amsden, and
stepson Matthew Landon; and to my stepson Tim Landon.*

*This book is also dedicated to the dear hearts out there,
who so welcomed and enfolded us.*

Contents

Preface

In May of 1998, when we were both in our midfifties, my wife, Lucia, and I took an amazing leap of faith. We moved from the urban Midwest we had inhabited for most of our lives to a home near the tiny town of Ramah, New Mexico, where we lived for the next twenty years. This book is a portrait of our life there, among an eclectic community of open-hearted, earth-rooted people. It is also an evocation of the deep spirit and history permeating Ramah, and of the necessity, central to the traditional beliefs of almost all Indigenous people, of living in concert with the needs of the earth.

Ramah is a small, rural town in northwestern New Mexico, in an area where Mormons farm amid the rhythmic yelp and drone of Native music, Penitentes sing ancient alabados, and old Spanish missions hunker above the bones of ancient people. Because it is also the name of the valley in which the town nestles, the lake nearby, and the closest Navajo reservation, Ramah is how we usually refer to this general area of the state.

Beside the town runs New Mexico Highway 53, an old, two-lane road that meanders west from Grants, New Mexico, to the Arizona border, serving as the main street for us and other people who live along its corridor.

Highway 53 has been designated by New Mexico as part of the Trail of the Ancients, because for hundreds of years Pueblo and nomadic tribes, Spanish and American explorers and settlers, and many others walked its route or rode horses, mules, or donkeys through the pine forests and volcanic flows it traverses. Now, internal combustion engines carry folks along the highway at speeds that would be unimaginable for those earlier travelers, past two national monuments, a national forest, and two Indian reservations.

Unlike in the suburban life we left behind, the natural world became a pervasive part of our daily existence. We built our home among ravens and steep-sided canyons and named it Cielo, Spanish for sky and heaven. Our nearest neighbors were ponderosas and white-tailed deer who reminded us daily of our tiny role in the great web of life. We were welcomed into a community where differences were more celebrated than criticized, and spadefoot toads sang of love in the land of the Zuni and the Navajo.

The cultural tapestry, the geology and natural history, the illumination of the sky and sunlight and brilliant night stars all give the area a deep and abiding energy. Even the most down-to-earth folks are aware of it; some people are so attracted when they arrive that they eagerly stay, while others are uncomfortable and eventually leave. For us we found the essence of our beloved querencia, our natural home, and developed a visceral belief in the potential to honor and accept all peoples as Natives, members of the first tribe of humans that arose in Africa so long ago.

New Mexico Highway 53

Gallup

Continental Divide

Cibola National
Forest

Grants

Zuni Mountains

Ramah Lake

Ramah

El Morro National
Monument

El Malpais National
Monument

53

Timberlake
Ranch

Ramah Navajo
Indian Reservation

Zuni

Zuni Indian
Reservation

53

36

602

40

40

ARIZONA

Navajo Indian Reservation

Acknowledgments

Many thanks to:

Lucia, my companion and lady of light who walked with me every step, experiencing, remembering, editing, encouraging, and enduring. Without thee it would not be.

Two people whose support and encouragement were key to the publication of this book. First, my editor, Michael Millman, who welcomed it into the University of New Mexico Press system, championed it throughout, and provided invaluable editing and advice.

Second, Jack Loeffler, for whom I have great respect as an implacable and iconic defender of the living earth. As one of the UNM early readers, he provided strong affirmation that buoyed both the book and me.

My early readers: Ed Packard for his invaluable suggestions and line-by-line guidance on content and form (we referred to format adjustment as "packardizing"); Roger Irwin, who helped me remember and improve this book throughout; Carla Van West, who provided crucial corrections of archeological terms, Native matters, and text; and Dana Letts, Deborah Singleton, Jim Parry, Reginah WaterSpirit, and Paula Sayword for their insight and blessings.

All the other UNM Press people who provided outstanding care and expertise. In particular James Ayers for his editorial, design, and production oversight; Felicia Cedillos, who designed the wonderful cover and designed and set the interior; and Min Marcus, who masterfully prepared, formatted, and copyedited the manuscript.

Nancy Dobbs for her splendiferous cover photo, which she took from her back door in the Ramah area.

Our family and friends who visited us there in our home beside the Trail of the Ancients.

All the people and places mentioned, and the ones loved but unmentioned. I am humbled and honored and blessed by you and grateful beyond measure so please, all of you, take a bow.

The wider community of souls in the Ramah area and out into northern New Mexico and beyond, those walking the earth now and those whose energies remain after their passing. When this book was first aborning it carried the title "Folk Music," and you were the ones to whom it referred.

Finally, the earth, our home, this beautiful, vulnerable blue marble. May we love her and help her regain her vitality and find our way to live together as the single human tribe we are.

1. Smallpox and a Ghost

WE BUILT OUR NEW home in a place called Timberlake Ranch, four miles of gravel and dirt roads east of Ramah, New Mexico. Ramah is a predominantly Mormon town, and its modern history began in 1876 when a small group sent by Brigham Young settled in the area. It was one of dozens of places in the southwest selected by him for Mormon settlement, and one of only two that remain. The Ramah settlers were instructed to perform missionary work among the Zuni and Navajo, and they named their first little community Savoia.

A year after Savoia was established, a family traveling with a wagon train of another group of Mormons took refuge from a winter storm in an empty adobe house clearly painted with the word "smallpox." Either because they couldn't read or because the weather gave them no choice, the family stayed in the house until the storm passed, and in the process became infected.

At some point the family rejoined the wagon train as it continued westward until reaching the settlement of Savoia, where the travelers briefly rested. After they left, the people of Savoia discovered they had in turn been infected with the deadly disease. During the bitter cold and heavy snows of 1878, smallpox ravaged the community, taking one person after another; mothers and babies, fathers and children were all struck down.

Because of the frozen ground, some of the bodies may have been buried in a hand-dug well. Several were interred in a small cemetery that still sits on the crest of a grassy hill above Ramah Lake. Enclosed today by a black wrought-iron fence and well-tended by descendants of the people buried there, the tiny grave-yard is tragic and eerie. In the early 1880s the people still living in Savoia left to form the town of Ramah a few miles to the south.

In 1912 Duane Hamblin, a former Arizona ranger, bought land, built a house not too far from the little cemetery with the smallpox victims, and moved there with his family. The Hamblin property was then sold in 1926 to Louis Dent, a man who had made his fortune as the owner of a string of movie theaters throughout Texas. He and his family named the place the Cloh Chin Toh Ranch and lived there for forty-two years. We were told stories about that time, of gather-ings and parties with show business people and other grand doings.

Eventually the Sanchez brothers, in partnership with a Califor-nia company called the Newport Group Investors, bought seven-thousand acres that included Cloh Chin Toh Ranch. After all the lots were sold, the developers gave up control and the board of directors of the newly created Timberlake Ranch Landowners Association took over. This is the short version of the history of where we built our home.

Now for a ghost story: Over the years some people claim to have seen the ghost of a girl whose body is buried among those who died of smallpox, in the little cemetery in Timberlake. Her name was Polly Ann Hamblin, and her tombstone says she lived from 1900 to 1918. The story goes that one cold morning, Polly informed her family that she was in love with a Navajo hand that worked on the ranch. Her father and brother became enraged and chased her suitor up the bluffs behind the house. Polly, distraught and still in her nightdress, followed them to try and save her love, but stum-bled and fell to her death.

Some folks say Polly's ghost haunts the old Hamblin ranch house that now serves as a meeting place for the Timberlake community. We heard numerous stories about encounters with her spirit, including the rattling of pots and pans in the kitchen at night and glimpses of her walking along the dirt road beside Ramah Lake.

We were told that one of the oldest remaining members of the Hamblin family called the story of Polly's tragic love and death nonsense. Polly, they said, died of "female difficulties." It seems to me, though, that ill-fated love could perhaps qualify as "female difficulties." In any case, a good ghost story is almost a necessity in a place like this, an enhancement of its abiding sense of mystery.

2. Off the Cliff

TO OUR FAMILY AND friends it might have seemed as if we just up and decided one day to move to the Ramah area, and our relocation actually went something like that. We engaged in almost no due diligence; no evaluation of the location for health care access, cultural opportunities, shopping convenience, or crime. We didn't review lists of "best places to retire" or seek input from anyone. We just knew where we wanted to be.

The move itself, of course, was much more involved. While our New Mexico house was being built, Lucia and I and our dog, Walter, lived in Kansas City, where I had resided since graduating from law school and where Lucia had spent most of her life. Our roots in the area were deep—I was born in Wichita, about 175 miles from Kansas City, and Lucia was a Kansas City native.

When some of our friends heard where we were going, they tried to talk us out of it. "You don't know anybody there," they said. "You'll be so isolated in the wilds of New Mexico." One predicted to Lucia that "You'll come right back." Others saw our move as brave and cheered us on. Our long-time friend Mary said something surprisingly helpful: "Because no one really knows you there, you can become anyone you want to be." That harmonized perfectly with our hopes and became an affirmation for us. We wanted to expand and grow into new experiences and vitality.

Lucia and I first met in the early 1970s as members of a group working toward the establishment of a Tallgrass Prairie National Park in the Kansas Flint Hills. We were married to other people then, and after the park was established as a national preserve and the environmental group disbanded, we didn't see each other for a long time. Over time our first marriages ended and our friend Lainey invited both of us to the opening of one of her photograph exhibits. We reconnected, fell in love, and eventually wed. By the time we moved to New Mexico we had been married for about six years.

Before we moved my job at the Kansas City regional office of the United States Environmental Protection Agency had gone from very satisfying to marching in place. I had worked with the agency since I graduated from law school and loved it for its mission and people, but I was ready for another chapter in my life. Lucia's work as a counselor no longer gave her much energy, and she also felt it was time to move on. Our life in Kansas City had grown old and familiar, and we both yearned for new experiences. I wasn't old enough, though, and didn't have enough years of service for retirement. Also, Lucia's elderly dad lived in Kansas City; we were his only family in town and we wouldn't leave him.

Then things gradually fell into place. Early retirement became a possibility and Lucia's dad entered his ninety-second year and gently passed away. I retired and Lucia closed her practice a couple of years later, just as our builder completed our home in Timberlake. Then we worked through the processes of selling our Kansas City house, packing our belongings, hiring two young men, renting a truck, and moving to New Mexico.

With all that our lives pivoted into something completely different, which always involves challenges. For me retirement was especially difficult. Before I retired I had a job and a title, and I got a regular paycheck. I knew what my weekdays would contain—when they would start and when they would end—and I felt good about my free time on evenings and weekends because I had worked hard and earned my rest. When people asked me, "What do you do?" I had an answer that identified me as an active contributor to society.

The period between my retirement and our move was empty and lonesome. I'd get up in the morning, kiss Lucia goodbye as she headed out into her day, and walk the dog past neighbors' houses where I'd see other busy people heading out to work. Then I'd go home and try to figure out what to do; I wanted to write but I couldn't seem to get anything started. Lucia went through some similar difficulties after she stopped working, but I think it was easier for her because by that time we were well into the busy moving process.

We had anxieties and cares after we moved to New Mexico, of course, but we would smile when we thought about the ways some of our friends in Kansas City might imagine our new lives: depressingly isolated or all carefree adventure. Sometimes when someone would call and ask me how we were doing, I'd say, "We're just living the dream." Although it was a joke, in many ways we really were.

Our decision to move was an amazing leap of faith—we knew surprisingly little about our new home. We had only met a few folks in the area and had no clue about how cold the winter nights could be, or that long power outages were part of the deal. We knew nothing about the contentious homeowner association, the bad roads during rainstorms, or the situations we would face such as a septic tank backing up on a windy New Year's Day with subzero temperatures.

This was probably a good thing, though, because if we'd known the full story, we might have remained in Kansas City and completely missed our adventure. Like Dorothy, we left beloved but familiar Kansas and landed in a bright new place, with the difference being that we found there our querencia, our heart's home.

3. Father John

BEFORE WE MOVED I worked for the US Environmental Protection Agency (EPA) in its Kansas City office. For one of my duties I served as the regional lawyer with Indian law responsibilities, which involved interacting on occasion with a man named John, who was a liaison between EPA and Indian tribes. John was a mixture of Delaware Indian and Irishman, and one of several people who quietly but significantly improved things at the agency. When I first met John I had no idea how he would open channels in me that would flow into our New Mexico home.

In some ways American Indian tribes have historically resembled the Balkans. They repeatedly made and severed alliances and fought and made peace with each other. Today the tribes still don't always agree on issues they share, but John believed that if they could unite around environmental principles, they would be able to expand their sovereignty and increase protection for the earth. He aspired to bring the tribes together in a coalition based on traditional Native American reverence for the natural world.

Although he was half Scotch-Irish, John identified completely with his Delaware side. He was a heavy-set man with braided hair, a deep, resonant voice, and an ability to not take himself too seriously. One summer John attended a meeting in Missouri of several tribes, and during a free afternoon he and a few other attendees took a boat out on Truman Lake. When a large bird flew out from the sun toward the boat, John said, "Look, an eagle!" They soon properly identified the bird as a turkey vulture and from then on, among those in the boat, vultures were referred to as Delaware eagles.

John took pride in the history of the Delaware people, whom he referred to as the Lenni Lenape, their name in the Delaware language. In their long history the Lenni Lenape once inhabited two-and-a-quarter million acres in eastern Kansas. He said his people are considered the grandfathers of the Lakota, and only the Seneca defeated them in battle. He described the treaty the US government signed with the Lenni Lenape as one of the first Indian treaties in the nation, as well as the first treaty to be broken.

His tribe was pushed here and there and had their land stolen again and again because their ownership interfered with the white man's "manifest destiny." And, in his gentle voice, he told me how his tribe of 15,000 people was reduced to a population of 1,400 in less than a century by blankets intentionally contaminated with smallpox, outright slaughter, and malignant abuse and neglect.

During John's many years as a policeman his fellow officers gave him the nickname "Father John" because he would sometimes take troubled young street people under his wing. His grandmother's gift of seeing things helped him locate stolen property and hidden weapons, and once led him to a corpse that had eluded everyone else. He survived violent confrontations that included gunfights and being stabbed, and he avoided the petty corruption that sometimes bleeds into the lives of police officers.

John talked at length about growing up with his medicine-woman grandmother and inheriting her gifts of intuition. He described hunting with his grandfather, passing through his middle life as a policeman in Kansas City, and reconnecting with his Native American heritage in his later years when he worked for

EPA. I would sit in John's government office cubicle beside his desk and become totally absorbed in his stories, something I did often, and I had no idea that he was weaving a dominant thread of interest into the next portion of my own life.

John was an important resource for me at a time when my sense of self was shifting. Talking to him was like taking on fuel; he had a calmness firmly rooted in his spiritual connection. I'd walk down the hallway, make my way through the maze of cubicles to John's place, and settle in. We'd sit there beneath the fluorescent lights and talk, and the bureaucracy would fade into his natural world.

John had a small, second-floor window beside his cubicle that he would open to put out bread and cracker crumbs for the pigeons. Their cooing would ease my mental transition to the settings of John's stories—the Oklahoma woods where he made hunting bows of ash wood, his grandmother's kitchen where she cried when she suddenly knew somehow that his father would soon die.

Around this time, Lucia and I became fascinated with New Mexico, taken with the energy and nature of the state. We often stayed in my sister and brother-in-law's little cabin adjacent to the national forest above Pecos, New Mexico, and took exploratory jaunts here and there. We also enjoyed bed and breakfasts, and a friend at work suggested we make our way to Ramah, New Mexico, and stay in the bed and breakfast there.

We did and were captivated, returning two or three times. We began thinking that if it weren't too expensive, we might purchase a little piece of land, and when we mentioned this to Nita, our hostess, she said in addition to running the bed and breakfast, she had just become a realtor. After showing us several lots, some tucked in pine-filled valleys and others on windswept hilltops, she took us to a spot in an area called Timberlake Ranch.

John knew we were looking for a place in the Ramah area to build a house. He hoped to come out to visit and bless our place, but he had become seriously ill, and we both knew that his illness made it unlikely that he could ever again be at an altitude of 7,200 feet. John had told me, however, of his connection to the hawk as his spirit animal. "When you see the hawk overhead," he said, "that is me. Watch for me." So when we arrived at the parcel of land we especially liked and saw a red-tail hawk circling overhead, we figured that was John, agreeing with our selection.

We bought the land, found a builder, and began the process of construction. John prayed over a twist of sage for us to use to bless our new home. He quietly held the sage for a while, squeezed it hard, then handed it to me, saying, "Take this to your new home, burn it while giving thanks to the six directions, and bury it." On our next trip we performed the ceremony and placed the ashes inside a cement block that would become part of a step from the hallway down to the living room. Sometime later, Ken, our builder, who knew nothing about John or our little ceremony, told us that when he was musing about some aspect of the house, he liked to sit on that step, right where we burned the sage. We never told him that perhaps John's blessing drew him there.

John and I were just beginning to put together a book on his extraordinary life when he died of congestive heart failure. Although he passed away before the completion of our house, his spirit would visit us out there. We now live in Albuquerque, but we still catch glimpses of him in the keening of a falcon or the eye of the Cooper's hawk who perches in the ash tree in our backyard. When I see him I still sometimes whisper, "Hello, John."

4. A Wedding in the Woods

SHORTLY AFTER WE MOVED to our new home we attended the wedding of a couple who lived in a tiny cabin in the woods near El Morro National Monument. The bride was the director of our local arts council and an artist, and the groom was a carpenter and telephone psychic—one of many people in the area with a unique flavor of some kind. A band played and beer and wine flowed freely. We remember that day as having a distinctive Woodstock vibe, a fine introduction to the diversity and creativity of our new community.

Gay men decked out in colorful drag danced in a circle in the backyard, and a man named Bear Heart, who would officiate, wandered around with a glass of wine in his hand, singing "On the Night We Were Wed." Bear Heart was an elder and highly respected Muscogee Creek medicine man, whom the groom referred to as grandfather. We have since learned that many people referred to Bear Heart as grandfather because they consider him their spiritual relative. Bear Heart performed a marriage ceremony Native American in nature, with circle prayers to the Great Spirit, a passed ceremonial pipe, and sage smudging to bring blessings on the joined couple and all of us gathered there.

Many other folks also attended, some all gussied up and others in their workaday garb. Despite the great variety in the group, everyone seemed to have an easy acceptance and affection for each other and the events going on around them. This seemed especially unusual for a sparsely populated rural New Mexico area where we expected conservative farming and ranching lifestyles as the norm.

As we waited in line on the front porch for the buffet we met a middle-aged man with a purple Mohawk haircut and large metal rings decorating his earlobes. We chatted a bit and found him intelligent and soft-spoken. His name was Eden and he had been in business of some kind before moving to a nearby gay communal retreat called Zuni Mountain Sanctuary.

The wedding took place at a cabin in El Morroville, an epithet some of us gave to the area containing the cluster of businesses and facilities along Highway 53 in the vicinity of El Morro National Monument. It includes two art galleries, a feed and grocery store, a Native arts trading post, a restaurant and lodging place, and, of course, the national monument itself. If Highway 53 was our main street, El Morroville was our downtown.

El Morroville's facilities include gathering places and performance venues. The Old School Gallery, for instance, is an art gallery and home to the local arts council. It has both indoor and outdoor stages and a full calendar that includes concerts, open mic nights, classes, and children's art shows. Beside the Old School Gallery sits El Morro Feed and Seed, which sells products like hay and chicken feed, locally made skin creams, and organic produce. Next to the feed store is Standing Feather's Galleria Carnaval, a small, richly stocked art gallery that includes Feather's own excellent paintings, along with books by local authors.

Directly across the highway you can find Pam and Jon's Inscription Rock Trading and Coffee Company. They sell bagels, smoothies, fresh coffee, and Zuni and Navajo arts and crafts, along with other treasures. The Rock, as some locals call it, has an outdoor patio and stage beside it with a dramatic red mesa as a backdrop.

We regularly enjoyed a variety of performances there, especially concerts by our local folk and blues band called the Billyhawks. Jon, the band's leader, is a former Nashville musician.

Sharron's Ancient Way Café stands adjacent to the Rock and features a restaurant, cabins, and RV hookups tucked among the trees. It also occasionally hosts performances, and El Morro National Monument just down the road offers full moon night hikes, Native artist days, stargazing, and other events.

Because the area experiences regular foot traffic, especially during the many festivals and community gatherings, several of us pushed the New Mexico Department of Transportation to reduce the speed limit on Highway 53 through El Morroville. Trucks regularly pull slowly in and out of the feed store, and people walk and drive back and forth across the highway from one venue to another. At this writing, additional roadside signs have been added, but the speed limit remains too high.

The anchor of El Morroville, El Morro National Monument, lies a mile or so east on the highway. At the heart of the monument is a massive sandstone bluff with a small perennial pool of fresh water at its base. Imagine how welcome that oasis has been in this high desert for travelers throughout the centuries, how it maintained the area as a primary respite and a good place to live. As long as two thousand years ago, ancestors of today's Zuni Indians made their homes in its vicinity.

About seven hundred years ago, hundreds of Zuni inhabited a pueblo of 875 rooms on the bluff's top. Their inscriptions, along with those from other tribes, conquistadores, priests, settlers, and a variety of travelers since, are among the two thousand carvings still visible along its base. The Zuni call the bluff A'ts'ina (place of writings on the rock), and the Spaniards called it El Morro (the headland). Today it is known in English as Inscription Rock.

The earliest European inscription is attributed to Don Juan Oñate, the first governor of the Spanish colony of Santa Fe de Nuevo Mexico. On April 16, 1605, he wrote three words that captured the essence of most Spanish inscriptions that followed: "Paso por aqui" (I pass through here). After the Spanish came the Anglo-Americans—soldiers and settlers and others who carved their name and usually a date, sometimes their origin, and occasionally a note on the purpose of their journey. Perhaps the most sought out by visitors is the inscription dated July 7, 1858, when Sallie Fox, a thirteen-year-old girl traveling with a wagon train going from Iowa to California, carved her name. She and her companions suffered many difficulties and privations on their journey, as described in Dorothy Kupcha Leland's popular children's book titled *Sallie Fox: The Story of a Pioneer Girl*.

To me the words and symbols on Inscription Rock have an almost visceral impact; looking at markings carved by people long gone gives a sense of physical connection. I feel the same connection while walking through the countryside and coming across a potsherd or a stone once used by Natives to grind seeds and grain. My connection to these artifacts feels even stronger because I know that I am almost certainly the only human to hold the item since its native creator hundreds of years ago.

During Teddy Roosevelt's presidency the historical significance of El Morro's inscriptions was so apparent that he designated it a national monument on December 8, 1906. In the words of William deBuys and our friend David Weber, co-authors of *First Impressions: A Reader's Journey to Iconic Places of the American Southwest*, "El Morro, still splendidly isolated, remains one of the Southwest's most iconic places. Indeed . . . it may be the very heart of the Southwest."

The monument features paths around the base of its bluff and spectacular views from the trail across the top, especially when the sunflowers are in full array. In some years the sunflowers are especially glorious; huge yellow swaths of them bloom everywhere in late summer. Some of the trails become so crowded with tall sunflowers that they create long, curving tunnels of bright yellow and green.

In this desert, where water is scarce and winters are long, we eagerly awaited the first wildflowers of spring. After winter abated each year we would watch for evening primroses, whose white, tissue-like blossoms were among the first to bloom. The orange spikes of Indian paintbrush appeared next, and then the flowers started coming on faster—purples, blues, reds and oranges, whites and yellows; we didn't know flowers came in so many different shades of yellow. I always watched for sweet sand verbena, the plant with my favorite flower name and an odd sour/sweet scent. Eventually we learned to identify and greet these blossoms and others as they joined the wildflower crowd.

Some of the wildflowers have special uses. The chamisa that streaks roads and hillsides with mounds of yellow blossoms in late summer, for instance, makes a vivid yellow dye. The roots of Rocky Mountain bee plants provide black pigment for Indian weavers and potters, and the stalks of Navajo tea can be dried to make a refreshing drink and a mild diuretic.

As the seasons progress from winter into spring, summer, and fall, the palette of blooming flowers expands like the gradual painting of a mural. By early September colors paint the hillsides and valleys as all kinds of flowers bloom together. People often visit the area in early autumn to experience the landscape at its most colorful.

Also, the mix of floral blooms differs every year. Variations in rainfall, wind, grasshoppers, and other factors mean some years are dominated by sunflowers, while others are marked by exuberant Rocky Mountain bee flowers, orange globe mallow, and other species. We don't remember which flowers were most abundant on that fall wedding day, but we do recollect our happiness when, as newcomers, we helped celebrate a wedding in a small cabin amid our first flowerful New Mexico autumn.

5. Folk Music

RAMAH IS A SMALL, picturesque town nestled in a bucolic valley. It is home to about 450 people, a Mormon church, a post office, one restaurant, and a couple of stores. Highway 53, which runs along its southern periphery, leads west to the Zuni Reservation and southeast to the Ramah Navajo Reservation. All around for miles and miles stretch forested hillsides and mesas sparsely speckled here and there with houses.

These homes belong to a diverse array of people. Many whom we hung out with were middle-aged hippies at heart, the kind of folks who spun wool, grew organic vegetables, and took on environmental issues. They loved to party and at Christmas you could expect invites to half a dozen gatherings, mostly attended by the same group traipsing from one house to the next.

I remember attending one of our first parties and the anxiety and mystery of driving in winter to a place we'd never been. We wandered through the dark on an unfamiliar dirt road for a long time, searching for the right house. We peered down side roads, trying to see if the homes faintly visible in the distance matched the description we had been given. We finally found the place, parked our car, and walked through the cold dark up to the door and into a toasty room full of welcoming people and the sweet fragrance of a piñon wood fire. The smell of burning piñon will always evoke memories of Ramah gatherings on winter evenings.

The number of artists we found in the Ramah area surprised us; creativity seems to fairly spring out of the countryside. Perhaps folks feel drawn to the rich cultural mélange or beautiful, high pine desert. Maybe the spirits of Native American ancestors have something to do with it. Whatever the reason, artistry is abundant. Many of the people who aren't artists in traditional ways engage in some other form of creation. They might stack cairns, raise bees, or garden organically. Labyrinths abound—we created one of our own out of fieldstone among a circle of tall pines behind our house.

The area has been aptly described as "like Taos before Taos became Taos," and perhaps the location of both communities in natural environments partly explains why. A 2017 study by the National Endowment for the Arts revealed that rural counties overlapping a forest or national park are almost 60% more likely to have a performing arts organization. This seems especially true in New Mexico.

The local gallery in the Ramah area is called the Old School Gallery, located in El Morroville. Although it is, of course, where local artists share and sell their work, the community also gathers there for a wide variety of other reasons. The gallery derives its name from the building's original purpose as a two-room schoolhouse in the 1940s. In those days children walked, rode horses, and, in the case of some Navajo living in the dorm in the nearby town of Mountain View, took a bus to and from the school. Both bus and school were heated with wood stoves, and the stove on the bus vented through a pipe in the center of the roof. Sometimes I imagine coming up behind the bus on the highway and wondering at its stovepipe with its wavering trail of smoke.

When the school closed in the 1950s the building was repurposed to store feed, grain, and hay. Later it housed wild west shows, and then it was used for storage again. After that it hosted gatherings, meetings, and the occasional dance. In 1998 it became the Old School Gallery and the home of the El Morro Area Arts Council.

Since then it has remained a space for art, poetry, theater, dance, and music. We always attended the quarterly art openings there, when the gallery displays new art and invites each artist to talk a bit about their pieces. The open mic nights were also fun; one occurred on the day our granddaughter Marz was born, and a Navajo folk singer sang her first "Happy Birthday" in the Navajo language.

Our hands-down favorite gallery happening was the winter solstice celebration, held on a Saturday night near the date of the astronomical occurrence. Eons ago humans performed ceremonies on the shortest day of the year to petition the gods to end winter, an example of a prayer that always worked. The Old School Gallery celebration takes place in the evening, often as snow falls outside, and it includes music, poetry, dance, and perhaps a short play written by someone in the community. After the celebration we would bundle up and gather outside around a fire, singing seasonal and folk songs. The evening was always packed.

Another popular event is the annual art show for students in the Ramah, Zuni, and Ramah Navajo schools. Many proud Navajo and Zuni family members attend show openings to celebrate the work of their children and grandchildren, including Navajo grandmothers resplendent in their long velveteen skirts and silver and turquoise jewelry.

We heard that the Navajo sometimes jokingly referred to the Old School Gallery as the white chapter house. Navajo chapter houses are similar to state capitols, and we occasionally traveled to the Ramah Navajo chapter house in the town of Pine Hill to vote or attend a meeting. The first votes we cast there took a long time because only a couple of voting booths were provided, and the ballot had to be translated line-by-line for those who only spoke and read Navajo. In later years more booths were provided and proceedings went much smoother.

The Ramah area also has its fair share of annual festivals and other doings, some taking place at the Old School Gallery and others involving much of the surrounding community of El Morroville. The largest event, the Ancient Way Fall Festival, pulls people from all over. Hundreds of folks pour in to buy art, crafts, and vegetables and listen to the music of the Billyhawks and other performers. The festival hosts contests for the most beautiful chicken, the ugliest vegetable, and the best homemade pie, and features kids' games, blacksmith demonstrations, and photography awards. Its many offerings change from year to year.

Many gatherings large and small also took place throughout the year at each other's homes. Some parties happened regularly: Kristi's mafia party, Will and Pam's ballroom dances, Jill's Scorpio gathering, and Kurt and Cindi's Fourth of July bash. Some were spontaneous; Dick and Claire would call in the afternoon with an invitation to dinner, which always led to an evening of comfort food and warm companionship.

We particularly looked forward to Jack and Sherri's Halloween celebrations. Jack was a fine poet and Sherri was a neon light artist, and both were master gardeners. Jack specialized in sweet corn and gladiolas he would arrange and bring to the farmers market, and the couple created together the gardens of flowers that surrounded their house.

Their Halloween parties sported many guests in full costume, and with so many artists in the community, that could really be something. Kristi was the runaway standout one year when she came as a witch with two faces, one dark and one light. She had painted an extra eye on each side of her head so when you looked at her right side you saw a completely white face, in contrast with her left side depicting a face that was completely dark. It was beautiful and vaguely disturbing.

On that night some folks danced to rock and roll and blues music while others sat or stood around the edges of the living room, chatting, drinking, and snacking on goodies. Pots of chili simmered on the stove, a piñon fire burned in the fireplace, and a few people sat outside and talked quietly around another fire. When the night grew late and we gradually began to leave, Jack walked each of us out with a flashlight, part of the way down the dark, narrow stone path that curved through their front gardens to the parking area. We fondly remember those winter nights when we left a gathering in a warm home filled with noise and companionship and moved into the cold, peaceful dark.

We looked forward to being with our friends and we looked forward to leaving too, driving down Highway 53, then on through the canyon and around the bluff faces shining in the star and moonlight, past the field with Mr. Pino's sheep to our curving driveway and into our garage.

The area is particularly blessed with gay folk; they are essential to the color, heart, and vitality of the community. When we first arrived we wondered why some of the gay men had names like Eden, Redwulf, and Standing Feather, and we were told that they were following a tradition to choose a name that better fit them than the one they were given at birth.

We saw very little intolerance for the differences among people, perhaps in part because the community is so small and varied. Our friends and neighbors could be opinionated and sometimes got into spats or even feuds, but never because of someone's skin color, sexual orientation, or religion. Even when people were mad at each other, they'd set aside their anger in an instant if someone needed help.

Wood was cut and stacked for older folks, roofs replaced when they blew off in storms, collections taken for families who lost their homes in fires. People were never ignored when stranded with their cars beside a road. This is one of the things I love about small communities: Neighbors depend on neighbors because they know and care about each other, partially due to there being no one else around. It's a great model for the world, as nations become more and more interdependent.

6. Glowing Bones

BEHIND A STAND OF tall ponderosas and scrub oak a mile or so from our house is a rock shelter, an area where the cliff has eroded and collapsed. With an opening much taller and wider than it is deep, the shelter is shaped somewhat like the half bowl of an amphitheater. A faint trail runs toward it across the grass, then curves up a small ridge through bushes, pines, and poison ivy to the entrance.

Against the back of the rock shelter stand a small, roofless stone room and a series of low rock walls. A jumble of stones and large boulders litter the floor, many of which fell from the roof long ago. It is an excellent habitation site: hidden, higher than the surrounding terrain, and out of the weather. A small group of Native people lived there eight or nine hundred years ago.

On the low ceiling toward the back you can see a faint, painted yellow turtle and some small handprints made by placing hands against the rock and blowing black powder around them. Smooth depressions in boulders where corn, pigments, or other foodstuffs were ground and holes used to sharpen sticks or tools evoke images of life there in the distant past. A person standing in the dim light of the shelter can look out its yawning mouth at the brightness of the blue sky.

Scattered about the interior are a few corn cobs, just two or three inches long, and some small potsherds. The corn cobs would normally have rotted away shortly after being discarded, but they survived in the protection of the dry rock shelter.

We would pause sometimes at the shelter entrance to tap on the cliff wall, just to listen to the clear echo. One evening we took some friends there for a meditation that included a recording of Native flute music and we were surprised at how the resonance enhanced and altered the sound. The rock shelter carried a definite sense of ancient habitation.

Katherine, a friend of ours, had moved to Timberlake and slowly built her house as she had the money. She told us that because she had worked for years as a nurse with area tribes she knew many people in the area, including an Indigenous salesman who had asked long ago for her advice. When Timberlake lots were first being sold, he would display a plexiglass box that contained items he'd found in the rock shelter. The box's contents included a moccasin, a sherd or two, and some small human bones.

He told her that one night, as he was driving back from a sales talk, something in the back seat began to glow. When he glanced back he saw that the glow came from the bones in the box. "I shouldn't be carrying those things around," he said. "I don't know what to do."

Katherine suggested he return the items to where he'd found them and said she would be glad to help. Together they carried the artifacts to a place beneath a large pine tree near the shelter, dug a hole, and buried them. She pointed the spot out to us while on a hike, and because we knew her as a practical person, we didn't doubt her a bit.

Katherine's tale reminded me of one I had heard from my old EPA friend, Father John. He told me that he and a Native friend were on a drive to deliver some sacred items to a tribe. The objects were being returned from a museum, as required by the Native American Graves Protection and Repatriation Act of 1990, a law that requires federal agencies and other institutions receiving federal funding to return certain items in their possession to culturally affiliated tribes and Native descendants.

John said that the artifacts they carried, which included human bones, were in a cardboard box in the back seat of the car, and as darkness fell, the box began to glow. "It was very eerie," he said, "but we were undisturbed because we saw it as an affirmation; the bones knew they were finally on their way home."

7. Flames and Fangs

IN MOST PLACES THERE occur particular natural events that strike fear in the hearts of residents. From floods to earthquakes to hurricanes, nature will find its way to rage. Wichita, where I grew up, for example, sits smack-dab in the heart of tornado alley. If a twister loomed, we knew to retreat to a storm cellar or a basement. We had tornado drills in schools and warning sirens placed all around town. When I was young a tornado flattened a large area on the edge of Wichita, and years later another tornado almost completely destroyed the town of Greensburg, Kansas.

In the Ramah area fires were our greatest threat. Abundant pine and cedar trees combined with a high desert climate mean fires occur regularly. They can flash into existence and grow quickly, threatening forests and homes. Luckily, though, Ramah firefighting is a combined, community effort, and it is done very well. When smoke appears on the horizon, folks are on it like ducks on a June bug.

One day a short while after we had moved to our new home, as we prepared to attend a potluck lunch, we looked out a window and were startled by the sight of billowing smoke less than half a mile away. We jumped in the car and rushed over to where the manager of our homeowners association, who had just happened to be passing by, was looping a tractor through the edges of the flames to make a fire break. Fire trucks soon arrived from both our volunteer fire department and the Zuni Tribe and put the fire out.

That was the first of many fires we saw through the years, fought by volunteer fire departments, US Forest Service firefighters, and the Zuni, sometimes all of them at once; the Zuni are particularly renowned for their fire-jumping and fire-fighting skills. Territorial feelings have no place in dealing with fires—everyone is threatened, and everybody is needed.

As if fires weren't dangerous enough, rattlesnakes are also common. Shortly after we relocated to Ramah we drove up the ridge overlooking Ramah Lake to look at a small house for sale for our friend Dana, who was also planning to move to the area. We got out of the car and when I walked to the house's gate to open it, I heard a clicking sound in the grass at the base of the gatepost. Thinking a cicada had made the noise I reached down, and just before I touched the grass I spotted a curled-up rattlesnake, tail aloft and buzzing, head pointed directly at my approaching hand. As I jumped away I heard a falsetto shriek that Lucia maintains came from me. I caught my breath and, standing well back, I gazed upon my first venomous New Mexico viper.

I like snakes—even rattlesnakes. When I see them on the road I stop and move them off to the side, but at that moment by the gate I performed my first rattlesnake leap. I suspect it happens when our lizard brains identify rattlers as imminent danger and jerk us away before our conscious minds can process what's going on.

I have since observed rattlesnake leaps a number of times, including once when Lucia and I were walking cross-country with Lucia's son Matt. Matt was leading the way down a hillside when he spotted a rattler in the gully bottom during his step across, prompting him to somehow instantly rise and move through the air. Lucia also once performed the rattlesnake leap from a sitting position when she found one curled beneath her lawn chair.

Rattlesnakes are pit vipers, which means they have pit depressions on their heads between their nose and eyes. The pits are highly sensitive heat sensors that help them locate prey in the dark, capable of detecting a difference of less than one degree. New Mexico has seven rattlesnake species, including the western diamondback, the massasauga, and the Mojave in the extreme south. The Mojave's hemotoxic and neurotoxic venom makes it the most dangerous; all the other New Mexico rattlesnakes have only hemotoxic venom.

Hemotoxic venom destroys red blood cells and causes swelling and general tissue and organ damage. The toxin works slowly enough, however, to allow for time to get medical help and receive a shot of antivenom. Neurotoxic venom, on the other hand, attacks the nervous system and can cause paralysis. It is deadlier and acts quickly, so a bite from a snake with neurotoxic venom may more likely kill you.

Lurid rattlesnake stories aside, they rarely bite humans. They don't want to bite creatures they see as threats, hence they have rattles. They would much rather scare you away with a noise than waste venom they need to capture their prey. We only knew of one person in our area who suffered a bite when she accidentally picked up a pile of leaves that contained a small rattler.

Despite these facts some people still fear rattlesnakes the most. Once, during a hike, we came across a neighbor who warned us that because of rattlesnakes we should never walk through the grass. We knew someone else who built two fences around their house, one inside the other, in an effort to keep rattlers out. It did not work; in fact, they seemed to have more rattlesnake visitors than anyone else. Because of our many encounters with rattlesnakes I finally did buy a snake stick to catch and carry them away if they came in the yard or close to the house, though I am kindly inclined toward them.

However, even I shiver at the way rattlesnakes overwinter. I had heard of rattlesnake dens and knew of people in the Ramah area who had them on their land, but I didn't give them much thought until I read about brumation, the word for how rattlesnakes hibernate. Rattlers clump together in underground dens through the winter, and they travel miles to return to the same den each year. They stay immobilized there until the weather warms, when they emerge together. Which brings me to the zinger: Sometimes a single den may hold as many as a hundred rattlesnakes. Having one of those in your backyard would definitely add anxiety to the arrival of spring.

When our grandson Silas was six or seven, he and I came across a rattler on a walk, curled and clacking away. As we stood and watched it, I told Silas that if he hears a rattlesnake but can't find it with his eyes, he should take a step and see if the rattling stops. If the rattle doesn't stop, he should backtrack and then take a step in a different direction, and continue doing so until he finds a safe passage. Silas stood still, stared at the rattler for a moment, then emphatically declared, "I want to go back to the house!"

Although rattlesnakes rarely bite people, they do occasionally bite dogs. Most dogs survive a bite, but some dog owners get rattlesnake aversion training for them anyway. Rattlesnake venom inoculation options also exist for dogs to reduce the likelihood of severe damage or death from a bite.

When we moved from Kansas City to rural New Mexico our dog, Walter, thought he'd died and gone to heaven. He had traded his small backyard for great spaces of field and forest and cottontails and jackrabbits by the score. Eventually a rattler bit him, but after a night at the vet's office with some antibiotics and antihistamines, he was fine.

Several years later, when he was fairly old, Walter got a second bite, this time on his lip, which he did not survive. The snake that bit him was hidden in the leaves on the side of the road during a walk he took with Lucia. He had run ahead of her when he suddenly yelped. Lucia never saw the snake, but there was no doubt about what had happened.

A couple of weeks after Walter died, Bear Heart and his wife,

Reginah, with whom we had become friends, came for a visit. After dinner the first evening we sat around the fire pit in our backyard. As we chatted, Reginah pulled a paper napkin from her purse that held meat from their lunch that day. Bear Heart took the meat, chanted a bit, and tossed it into the fire as a blessing for Walter, and as permission for his spirit to move on. Then he brought tears to Lucia's eyes when he told her, "He was protecting you. He took the rattlesnake bite so you wouldn't."

In addition to rattlesnakes there are a few "imposters," such as the bull snake, which is patterned like a rattler and will also shake the tip of its tail to enhance its disguise. One way to differentiate rattlers from pretenders involves looking at their pupils. Rattlesnake pupils are elliptical like the eyes of a cat, while nonvenomous snakes will have round pupils. This is not a test, however, for the fainthearted or shortsighted.

When I was a boy my father and I were walking along a Kansas creek when we came across a hog-nosed snake, one of my favorites because of its trickster nature. It looks like a small rattlesnake except that it has no rattle, and the tip of its nose turns up. Although it is harmless, fussing with it will make it hiss like a cobra, shake its tail like a rattlesnake, and if neither of those fakes scares you away, it will lie on its back with its mouth open, pretending to be dead.

Imposters and rattlers aside, the western coral snake reins as the most venomous snake in New Mexico. They reside only in the far southwestern corner of the state, are nonaggressive, and often do not grow large enough to bite, but because of their venom's potency watch out for them when in their territory. They have red, yellow, and black bands, but so do other snakes, so it helps to remember this little ditty: "Red touches yellow, kills a fellow; red touches black, a friend of Jack." Or maybe you should avoid any snakes with colored bands, in case you don't have the ditty quite right.

8. First People

LIKE OTHER INDIGENOUS PEOPLE around the world, traditional American Indian communities can be very different from the rest of the country, with their own languages, nature-based cultures, and religions. And many of them have genetic lineage that extends back thousands of years, to the people who first inhabited this continent. The pervasive presence of Native Americans in New Mexico plays a large part in the state's identity as one of the most fascinating in the nation.

Growing up in Wichita, Kansas, in the fifties and sixties, our textbooks only discussed Indians in relation to the wars they fought against the US Army and their resistance to the spread of settlers. That and what we gleaned from Western movies and TV shows were all that most of us knew about them. We did not have readily available information about their long history. We certainly didn't know that when the first Europeans arrived on this continent they encountered an array of highly developed societies and governments.

Our teachers didn't tell us that the Great Law of Peace of the Iroquois Confederacy was an important model for the documents that defined the values and structure of our new country, including the US Constitution itself. The Great Law of Peace was a Native constitution that existed for hundreds of years before Europeans arrived. It contained 117 articles that assigned governmental roles to each of the six Native nations that ratified it. In 1988 Congress memorialized the importance of this law and other Native contributions to the creation of our government by adopting a resolution that stated in part:

> Whereas the drafters of the Constitution, including most notably, George Washington and Benjamin Franklin, are known to have greatly admired the concepts, principles, and governmental practices of the Six Nations of the Iroquois Confederacy; whereas the Confederation of the original thirteen colonies into one Republic was influenced by the political system developed by the Iroquois Confederacy as were many of the democratic principles which were incorporated into the Constitution itself. . . . The Congress . . . acknowledges the contribution made by the Iroquois Confederacy and other Indian Nations to the formation and development of the United States . . .

Hopefully, as we move toward a more informed and appreciative understanding of Native peoples, the stereotypes to which they are often subject will fade away. Before we moved to New Mexico I read a newspaper article about a young Navajo man and his frustration with the stereotypes he faced. It seemed to him that white people often see Indians as either alcoholics or sages. "All I'm trying to do," he said, "is get an engineering degree."

American Indians are as varied as any other group. Some live deeply in their traditional ways, while others do not. According to the Indian Health Service, only 22 percent of American Indians live on reservations.

American history did not begin with the arrival of Spanish and English explorers; it began much earlier with the ancestors of today's Native people. They were the first humans to populate North America, and they came from Asia.

The continent closest to North America isn't South America but Asia—the land masses of Siberia and Alaska are just fifty-three miles apart at the Bering Strait. Technically, in fact, the United States and Russia sit even closer together, separated by less than three miles because of two islands in the middle of the Bering Strait, one of which belongs to Russia and the other to the US.

Scientists have long believed that there, at the Bering Strait, humans first entered North America, over a land bridge that for three million years repeatedly appeared and disappeared as sea levels fell and rose. Human migration would have occurred during the last ice age, when glacier formation allowed the bridge to emerge. The bridge has remained covered by water since the ice age ended.

Although the land bridge was perhaps the primary way humans came to this continent, people also travelled a variety of other paths, along coastal routes or across oceans, and they first arrived long before we previously believed. Recent archeological research revealed that the ancient footprints found at White Sands National Park in New Mexico may be the oldest evidence of humans anywhere in the Americas, dating back some twenty-one thousand to twenty-three thousand years.

Whatever the dates and pathways, the first people to inhabit the Americas were Asian in origin and their descendants are among today's American Indians. As of this writing, 567 federally recognized tribes exist in the US, about half of which have a reservation. Indians constitute less than 2 percent of the US census–determined population, a statistic somewhat difficult to nail down when the criteria set by each tribe for membership vary.

New Mexico has twenty-three federally recognized Indian tribes: nineteen Pueblo tribes, three Apache tribes, and a portion of the Navajo Nation, with Native peoples making up 10 percent of the state's population. In the area where we lived most Native Americans are Navajo or Zuni.

9. Horses Coming Home

HORSES ORIGINALLY EVOLVED IN North America between three and four million years ago before spreading into Asia and Europe, probably by crossing the Bering Strait. Then they became extinct here some ten thousand years ago, until they returned with the Spanish. When Cortes, Coronado, De Soto, and the other conquistadores brought horses to this continent in the early 1500s they were just bringing them back home.

A Spanish royal decree required that all the earliest ships headed to the New World from Spain carry horses, and the trip for them was long and difficult. An area in the Atlantic Ocean en route to the Americas had unreliable winds, often rendering ships becalmed. If the ships were delayed too long and the supplies necessary to keep the horses alive were exhausted, sailors had to throw the animals overboard. This is why the area is now called the horse latitudes.

Mustang, the word used to describe the descendants of those Spanish horses, derives from the Spanish for "wild" or "stray." In some parts of the United States the term applies to any wild horse, but in the Southwest mustang usually only refers to horses descended from those originally brought from Spain. Spanish mustangs have relatively small builds, stocky legs less likely to break from missteps, and good reputations for their stamina and nature. They are the forebears of cowboys' preferred horses, the horses ridden by Indian warriors, and the mounts of the US Calvary.

Joty, a man who lived not far from us in Timberlake Ranch, so loved mustangs that he developed a herd of them as genetically close as he could to those brought over centuries ago, and we often saw them in his pasture near Ramah Lake. They reminded us of the Ian Tyson song "La Primera" that celebrates their history, and after we gave a copy of the song to Joty, he had it played over PA systems when his mustangs entered the arena at horse shows.

The mustang makes up a large component of the herds of free-running, feral horses that exist today, especially in the West, and this country has long wrestled with the proper way to manage them. Should they be protected as native wildlife or should they be captured and removed from public lands because they are the progeny of escaped or released domesticated animals?

Congress responded to the dilemma of feral horses on federal property in 1971 by enacting the Wild and Free-Roaming Horses and Burros Act. This law declares wild horses and burros as "living symbols of the historic and pioneer spirit of the West" and designates the Department of Interior and US Forest Service as responsible for the management, protection, and study of unbranded and unclaimed horses and burros on federal land. The State of New Mexico provides similar statutory protection to feral horses on state lands and extends additional protections to Spanish mustangs.

Some years ago we were driving down a two-lane New Mexico highway when we noticed a herd of a dozen horses running along the fence line beside the road. There were no cross fences, just wide-open rangeland that stretched to the horizon, and a herd of what we assumed were feral horses began galloping beside us. We drove with them for a couple of miles, then pulled over to watch them disappear into the distance. We have never forgotten that experience. It felt like the difference between looking at zebras in a tiny zoo enclosure and watching them run freely through their natural expanse.

Nobody knows exactly how many feral horses and burros exist in this country today. The US Department of the Interior manages about eighty-eight thousand of them, and the US Forest Service has something less than ten thousand. American Indian tribes also have them under their stewardship, especially the Navajo Nation, with an estimated population of forty thousand.

Burros also arrived with the early Spaniards and are of the same ancient Equus line from which the horse evolved. Maryanna and Kathleen, who lived a few miles away from us, sometimes take in wild or abandoned horses or burros and give them food and medical care. They were particularly fond of an old burro named Ruben, who had an abundance of personality and self-esteem. He joined their family as part of a horse/dog/burro trio they came across, a trio of previously mistreated creatures.

A couple of bands of wild horses roamed in our vicinity, one on Mount Taylor near Grants, New Mexico, and another outside the town of Placitas near Albuquerque. We never saw those herds, but whenever we wandered up into the golden realm of fall aspens on Mount Taylor, we kept our eyes out for them.

10. Wave Riding

OUR EXPERIENCES EARLIER IN life can sometimes surprise us by being good preparation for what comes later. You'd never imagine, for instance, that working for the US Environmental Agency would be useful training for living in a small, rural community.

I had just graduated from law school and it was my first day working for Region VII of the US Environmental Protection Agency in Kansas City, the organization responsible for implementing several federal environmental laws in the states of Kansas, Missouri, Iowa, and Nebraska. Jack Morse, my boss and a man who would become a dear friend, handed me a copy of a complex statute that had recently been enacted, the Federal Water Pollution Control Act Amendments of 1972. He said, "This is your baby. Study it, read through its legislative history, and get ready for questions from the program managers and engineers and biologists you'll be working with."

The law he placed in my hands was a comprehensive rewrite of the existing national system that protected the quality of water in this country. The new statute required the establishment of water quality standards for each lake and river and the implementation of a permit program controlling every discharge of pollution from factories and other sources into the waters of the nation. It also addressed nonpoint sources of water pollution, such as agriculture, landfills, and construction, and authorized states and Indian tribes to assume water protection authority if they developed sufficient laws and procedures.

I was just a wet-behind-the-ears kid, but the law was new to everybody, so we all kind of had to start from the beginning to create a system that would really work. And it wasn't just us at EPA; many other folks with different stakes were involved in the process. States, Indian tribes, cities, environmental groups, industries, farmers, and universities all played a role, and it was exhilarating to imagine, assemble, and implement our new and improved water quality protection system. All along the way we encountered frustration, controversy, and compromise, but the results wouldn't have been as good without these hurdles.

Jack believed lawyers were most effective when present while decisions were made. For me that meant I frequently went out with the technical staff to their national meetings, and often I was the only regional attorney there. I accompanied them on state visits and worked with them day-to-day as they drafted protocols, made program decisions, and worked through thorny issues. As a consequence, I developed an understanding of the scientific and practical aspects of our work, which made me more useful to the programs and more personally invested in the work.

Later on, because of the amendment of another federal law, each regional EPA office had to form a department of groundwater protection. Office leadership asked me to become the director of ours in Region VII, so I put on a program management hat and pulled together a small team to focus on groundwater. And off we went, cooperating, battling, and negotiating, participating in the creation of another major chunk of environmental protection.

When Lucia and I moved to the Ramah area we encountered similar communal efforts. Organizations to address community needs were developing or shifting and they needed help. The diversity of people in the community meant we had to consider an abundance of different perspectives, interests, and rigidities. In addition, because of the small population base, we had to function, to some extent, as Jacks and Jills of all trades. My work at EPA equipped me well for these situations, and the first call for help came before we had even moved.

While we finished our packing in Kansas City, one of our future neighbors called and asked if I would be willing to join the Board of Directors of the Timberlake Ranch Landowners Association, a homeowners association that included our new house. "It's no big deal," he said, "just meetings once a month about minor stuff. It won't take a bunch of time."

"Okay," I replied, though, unbeknownst to me, that "okay" was like Hansel smiling at the witch as she led him to the oven.

Timberlake Ranch is a residential area that covers 7,000 acres and is partially surrounded by 342,000 acres of the Cibola National Forest. It contains 743 lots, each of which is five acres or more, and extends into two counties. Almost a fifth of its area is commons: areas owned jointly by all landowners, such as the ranch house and the roads and land around part of Ramah Lake. Only about twenty percent of the lots had homes, and the others were owned by people who only came out occasionally or didn't come to the area at all.

The association collected dues, enforced rules, paid bills, paid taxes, oversaw a couple of employees, and communicated with its members about elections and issues. That all seemed pretty straightforward until we attended our first annual meeting when I was considered for the board.

The meeting was held in the Timberlake volunteer fire station. We got there a little late and walked into a room already full of people who were popping up and down and yelling at board members and each other while the president tried to establish order. We watched this for a little while, then looked at each other with the same question in our minds: "Is this really a good idea?" Good idea or not, the association elected me to the board for a three-year term, and I suddenly found myself in a group of folks riding runaway ponies as hard as they could in different directions.

Over the next three years our board worked hard to settle disagreements and overcome challenges, including a lawsuit filed by a disgruntled landowner that involved my being legally served in the middle of an annual meeting. That suit sought dissolution of the entire homeowners association and we almost lost, but we finally prevailed. We faced plenty of other scuffles and discord, but we gradually established better ways of running meetings, supervising employees, and budgeting.

After I became board president I convinced our friend Roger to join the board by using the same lie on him that was used on me. I told him, "Being on the board is no big deal." To this day, Roger, who became board president after me, reminds me of the chicanery I used to rope him in, but in jest; he was as happy to be of service as was I.

After Roger and I both served on the board, and as the association seemed to function smoothly, another unhappy landowner decided he wanted to run things his own way. He secretly got proxies from several nonresident landowners, brought the proxies into an annual meeting, and used them to vote himself and some of his cronies onto the board. He then became president and began operating like a despot, making destructive decisions and acting in violation of the bylaws. He took major actions without board knowledge or approval, tried to break the association up into several smaller ones, and finally stopped holding board meetings completely, among other things.

A group of us who opposed his actions formed a coalition to do what we could to change things, meeting at various people's homes. Roger created a website to get information out to the landowners so they could understand the situation. We complained to the New Mexico Attorney General's office and anyone else who would listen. A New Mexico district court finally appointed a mediator to try to resolve matters, and he held several contentious meetings in a futile search for common ground. Eventually, most board members serving under the then president became disgusted and resigned, the troublemaker left the area, new board members took over, and the organization settled into normal operation again.

Managing a rural homeowners association may seem like a simple thing, but from my experience, nothing could be further from the truth. This applies especially to our case because Timberlake Road, the only access into our area, passes through Indian country.

My EPA Indian law experience left me with an enduring appreciation for the labyrinthine complexity of jurisdictions in Indian country. Tribal, federal, state, and county authorities overlap and vary significantly from tribe to tribe. In addition, Indian country has many different land ownership categories, including land owned by tribes, held in trust, owned by individual Indians, and owned by non-Indians.

Finally, there is the complication of checkerboarding, where Native land and non-Native land intermingle. Part of the Navajo Reservation that lies in northwestern New Mexico, where we lived, particularly faces this problem. Checkerboarding has several causes, such as grants to railroad companies of land along their tracks, sometimes in alternating sections, originally given as subsidies in the late 1800s. Checkerboarding complicates jurisdictional issues, creates community conflicts, and makes it difficult for the Native nations to effectively manage and use their land for agricultural or other purposes.

We ran head-on into this issue when a group of us in Timberlake sought improvement of Timberlake Road, the dirt and gravel passageway that crosses Navajo trust land on the way to our homes. The road extends north from Highway 53 for several miles and runs through our area and on into the Box S Canyon. In addition to the trust section where the US Bureau of Indian Affairs (BIA) and the Navajo Tribe hold sway, the road crosses portions of two different counties, and most of it serves as a US Forest Service road as well.

Part of the road was graveled, and part was not. Some areas

became flooded mudholes or sand traps. Grading and maintenance occurred sporadically here and there by the two counties, the Timberlake Landowners Association, or not at all. A small section received coverage by an agreement that required the county to provide gravel and Timberlake to provide maintenance, and jurisdictions shifted throughout. It was a mess.

When we finally managed to get all the actors together, they mostly denied responsibility at first, pointing at each other and saying, "It's their job." This sounds like a criticism, but it is not. Each of these organizations constantly has to stretch their small fiscal resources across many needs, and we were asking them to assume additional burdens. Eventually, though, after several meetings, a pragmatic solution emerged.

Timberlake has fared fairly well for several years now, in part because we all learned the hard way that failure to pay attention to the happenings in our community can have undesirable consequences. The experience was good, but I told Lucia to just shoot me if I ever talked about serving on a homeowners association board again.

All this illustrates one good aspect of moving to a small community: Organizations often have dire need of warm bodies to pitch in and do things. As a result, they welcome newcomers and pull them into this and that group where they can get to know their neighbors and make a difference. We discovered that the Old School Gallery housed another of these organizations eager for help.

Art, Native and otherwise, is integral to the heart and economy of New Mexico. We knew art thrived in bigger cities like Santa Fe and Taos, but we happily discovered that many small communities, such as the one in the Ramah area, teem with artists as well. As mentioned earlier, a group of local artists had set up an art gallery in the old school building close to El Morro National Monument, named it the Old School Gallery, and created the El Morro Area Arts Council (EMAAC) to run it. EMAAC needed people to serve on the board and do a myriad of other tasks, so Lucia and I both became involved.

Around this time, someone suggested that before we went too far it might be a good idea to develop an understanding of what we all envisioned for EMAAC and the gallery. Everyone agreed, so a bunch of us gathered one day to come up with a mission together. The original idea was to have a communal art gallery to sell the works of local artists, but we soon realized that if the gallery provided only this service, most of us who weren't artists wouldn't have much interest or reason to volunteer. If, on the other hand, the gallery served a wider variety of purposes, we'd all be eager to pitch in.

The little, one-room schoolhouse already had a stage that could host plays and musical performances, and people suggested that it would also be a great place for dances, workshops, concerts, and meetings. As the possibilities flowed out and the excitement grew, the group realized what a treasure we had. On that day the Old School Gallery blossomed into an integral part of the community with festivals, dances, workshops, dramas, poetry readings, and art shows for kids.

A few years after that, I served on the committee that evaluated all the arts councils in New Mexico for state funding. We rated each council numerically, and I was proud of EMAAC for always ranking among the highest, primarily because of the wide variety of activities we did and the broad involvement we had across our community.

When we think about creativity we tend to imagine people engaged in solitary pursuits: the writer at her desk, the painter in his studio, the composer at their piano. Often, though, creativity is much broader. Efforts by groups of people working in concert to develop new environmental programs, improve a homeowners association, or work with a newly born arts council are every bit as creative. These groups are like orchestras—folks getting together with a common goal, fumbling around, tuning instruments, and feeling their way until they gradually create harmony.

11. Blue Bird Flour

A FEW MILES WEST of El Morro National Monument, Highway 53 swings around a hill and suddenly a wide canopy of trees appears, pierced by the white steeple of the Mormon church. There stands the town of Ramah, looking from the distance like a tiny New England community. The highway continues along the edge of town, past the Stagecoach Cafe and the post office, and then, just where the speed picks up again, a road turns off to the right and leads to the home of two of the most gracious and interesting people we knew.

At the end of the road Patti and Paul Merrill lived on several acres of land, with a horse named Pepper and two dogs named Shadow and Trouble. Paul was of slight stature, bald and thin and straight, with the thick-fingered hands of a man who has worked physically all his life. Patti was diminutive and bright as a penny, and they each beamed with pleasure when visitors arrived.

Both were born in Ramah; Paul grew up in a little house in the center of town and Patti's childhood home was three or four blocks away. Paul was raised a Mormon but Patti was not. When World War II broke out Paul left to join the Marines, became an officer, and served five years in the Pacific theater, including a station in

Pearl Harbor when the Japanese bombed it and catapulted this country into the conflict. After the war he returned to marry Patti and they moved to Fort Wingate, a small New Mexico community adjacent to a defunct army fort and munitions depot.

Fort Wingate is about sixty miles north of Ramah and where the couple spent the next forty-five years while Paul operated a trading post and an automobile dealership. Both enterprises did business primarily with the Navajo from the nearby reservation. Then they moved back to Ramah in 1991, closing the circle of their homes together at a distance only about sixty miles in diameter. Which doesn't mean they never went farther than that; in fact, they traveled the world.

A natural storyteller, Paul had a host of tales to share. One day we were talking about the different ways people held funerals and he told me about attending the service for a friend of his who was a highly respected Navajo man. "His funeral was like nothing I have ever seen," he said. "He was buried with great ceremony, and with the body of his horse."

He also had some great stories about selling cars and trucks to people from the Navajo community, and how the experience differed from selling vehicles elsewhere. "For one thing," he said, "rather than the usual monthly payments, Navajos would often make two big payments a year. One would be in the spring when the lambs were born, and the other in the fall when the sheep were shorn. That's when they had the money, and that's when they would pay."

Before he sold cars Paul sold horse-drawn wagons. At one point he decided to take back some of the wagons he had sold previously, in trade for cars and trucks. After he put ads on the Navajo radio station he found himself flooded with trade-in wagons.

When I asked what he did with the wagons he said, "Well, I sold most of them to movie producers in Hollywood. They were loaded up on semitrucks and hauled to California to use in Western pictures. If you watch an old John Wayne movie and see horse-drawn wagons being attacked by Indians, you can appreciate the irony. There is a good chance the wagons had once been owned by Navajo Indians in New Mexico."

The countryside around Fort Wingate is spectacular, with mesas whose tops give panoramic views of the distant stair-step hills and plains. Some evenings Paul and Patti would load a pickup with steaks and friends and follow a tortuous path to the crest of one of the highest mesas in the area. There they would build a big fire, cook the steaks, and enjoy the night air.

After dinner, when darkness had fallen and they were ready to go, they would push the red coals over the edge and watch them cascade down the mesa face. Paul would have placed an especially large log in the fire earlier, and as a finale he pushed it, glowing with coals, over too. It would hit and break into bright chunks as it fell, and those would break into many more until the stream of fiery embers tumbling down the mesa created a long, bright trail.

Then they all piled into the truck and carefully picked their way down in the New Mexico night. "The people who lived along there got so they would know what was going to happen," he said, "and as they saw us passing their homes on our way up, they would come out and sit in their yards and wait for the light show."

Shortly after we met Paul and Patti, they decided to acquaint us with fry bread, a staple in the Navajo diet, so they invited us to their house one evening for a fry bread experience. We walked a short distance out to where they had a campfire going, with a cast-iron Dutch oven suspended above it on a metal hook. The pot held four cups or so of Crisco, nice and hot. "The oil has to be hot enough," Patti said. "You can tell it's ready when a small piece of dough dropped into the pot sizzles and begins to immediately cook."

Their Navajo friends taught them the proper way to cook fry bread when they lived at Fort Wingate. In the early days folks cooked it in mutton tallow or pig fat, then lard became the oil of choice. Now, because of convenience and health reasons, most people use Crisco. I never imagined that one day I'd hear Crisco referred to as a health food.

To fry bread experts the choice of flour is important, and Paul's Fort Wingate trading post sold flour that his Navajo customers preferred. It was milled especially for him in Liberal, Kansas, and he would buy ten thousand pounds at a time. Today the preferred flour is a brand called Blue Bird, and grocery stores all over Navajo country sell it. It comes in large, white cloth sacks with a picture of a blue bird on the front. The bags are pretty, and some folks sew them into aprons and other items to sell to tourists.

We each made our own fry bread that evening by tearing off a hunk of dough about the size of a large egg and working it back and forth between our hands until it was very flat and thin. Then we punched a hole or two in the center to help it cook well on both sides and dropped it into the hot grease. We turned it over once, removed it when it was golden brown, and drained the excess grease on paper towels.

Adding honey or powdered sugar made them delicious, kind of like thick sopapillas, the traditional treat served at the end of a meal in a Mexican restaurant. Without sweetener, fry bread traditionally accompanies stew or soup. Songs and bumper stickers extol fry bread's wonders, and it appears on tee shirts and hats.

Fry bread had its beginnings in adversity. When the Navajo were held captive at Fort Sumner in New Mexico in the 1860s, they created fry bread as a way to eat government rations of flour. Today it is one of the most ubiquitous Native American foods, served by tribes across the country at powwows and other gatherings. A proposal even arose to make it the state bread of New Mexico, but nutritionists and others who feared that it would exacerbate the epidemic of diabetes among Native people defeated the idea.

Beside Paul and Patti's house Paul had a large workshop where he built and restored things, including old horse-drawn wagons. He was particularly proud of an 1884 US Army wagon he completely renovated and drove in the annual Ramah Pioneer Day Parade each July 24, pulled along by his horse, Pepper, as he waved to all his friends and neighbors. The event celebrates the day Brigham Young entered the Salt Lake Valley in 1847, and the day is an official holiday in Utah.

Besides Utah, Mormons came to Ramah from elsewhere. In the early 1900s, for instance, a group of Mormons arrived from Casas Grandes in Mexico, where they had fled to avoid the laws of the United States that made bigamy illegal. Even though bigamy remained illegal, many of them later returned because rebellion in Mexico made living there too dangerous.

Patti had relatives among those from Casas Grandes, and they would sometimes tell stories about living in Mexico. "They lived fairly communally, and often didn't have enough food," Patti said. "When children were hungry and food was scarce, adults would give them stale bread from the communal stores. They would throw the bread into the irrigation canals and then run downstream and fish it out after it had softened." Patti and Paul once took a trip to Casas Grandes, and Patti recounted the strange experience of seeing houses in Mexico that looked like they had been plopped down from somewhere in the Midwest United States, occupied by Mormons who spoke no English.

Perhaps the most enduring legacy of Paul and Patti is the Ramah Museum, an old stone house filled with historic memorabilia from the people of the community. Paul and Patti conceived the idea, obtained the building, pulled together the resources to renovate it, and gathered the collections from their friends and neighbors. Because of their efforts the New Mexico Department of Cultural Affairs presented them with a New Mexico Historic Preservation Award in 2004. All their lives, both dedicated themselves to making their community better.

When we took walks down the central street in Ramah, where

the parades and the summer farmer's markets were held, we would pass the Ramah Museum and think about Patti and Paul. Sometimes we spotted a long black feather in the Ramah Museum yard, a reminder of the vultures that roost during the summer in the large trees that shade the building. Each year, after the vultures return from Mexico, where they spend their winters, for some reason they prefer to roost in those particular trees.

The ravens also like that spot; we'd hear their chuckles and croaks as they hid in the branches and crane our necks to see who could spot them first. I once asked Paul about the history of the great Ramah trees, startling adornments for such a small desert town. He told me that although at first glance they look like cottonwoods, they are poplars. Their leaves are green on top with bottoms so pale they are almost white. When the wind blows the trees shimmer like aspens. They are huge sentinels along the streets, deeply crenulated trunks rising high into wide-spread crowns. This is what he said about their history:

> They came to Ramah from Joseph City, Arizona, in 1882, carried in one five-gallon bucket. Imagine having to worry about water for families, horses, and stock, and also for a bucket of trees. Imagine, too, how few and small the trees must have been to all fit in there. All the massive poplar trees in Ramah today came from the small starts in that single bucket.

He went on to list the three varieties of poplar: Lombardy, Carolina, and silver leaf. Some were planted around the old log cabin built on an Indian ruin at the corner of Bloomfield and McNeil Streets. The home that eventually replaced the log cabin became the Merrill Hotel, a boarding and rooming house and the place where Paul grew up. It is now on the National Register of Historic Places.

In the early 1900s Bob and Giles Master came from England to start a trading post in Ramah and brought black locust trees for their home site. They planted the black locusts for shade and because their hardwood was good for making wagon and farming parts, such as doubletrees for harnessing horses and handles for tools.

The early trees grew tall because of the irrigation ditches throughout Ramah that carried water from nearby Ramah Lake. Though the trees no longer receive water from those ditches, they still tower majestically throughout the town.

Paul and Patti gave our grandsons Kenny and Nate their first horseback rides, and they always asked Kenny to play the Marines' Hymn on their piano when the kids visited. A few years later, during a visit from Lucia's son Tim, his wife, Beth, and their children, Silas and Marz, they gave Silas and Marz their first horseback rides too.

They took us to cut Christmas trees, shared meals with us, and sometimes Paul even drove their grader out to clear our road after a particularly big snowstorm. When they passed away their absence left a very big hole in a very small town, and in our lives too.

12. The Casket Makers

PAUL MADE CASKETS. HE didn't get paid for it and he didn't particularly like it, but he did it. He was about eighty when his beloved wife, Patti, lay dying in their home at the base of a mesa marked with petroglyphs and thin, black seams of coal. He fashioned her casket in his workshop beside their house and when he completed it his daughter lined it with a Pendleton blanket. Patti passed, they held her funeral, and over the next month or so Paul surrounded her grave with a beautiful wall and benches made of stones from their land and planted upon the surface a bed of wildflowers. On the wall he put items she cherished, cementing them among the stones.

A couple of years later we visited Paul one day and found him in his workshop fashioning another casket, this one tiny. When we asked whom it was for, he explained that one of his grandchildren was expecting a baby that the doctors were sure would die very shortly after birth. As the doctors predicted, the casket was needed.

Then Paul eventually married again, this time to a lady named Flora. Once, we visited them when Flora was mourning the recent death of her closest lifelong friend, and Paul was in his workshop crafting her casket just in time for her internment.

Paul wasn't the only one who made caskets in the area. Our neighbor Dorn made a casket for Katherine, a lifelong crusader. Among other things, her causes included opposing power line construction through the nearby national forest and stopping developers from building homes in the Timberlake commons beside Ramah Lake.

Katherine was organizing a yard sale to help raise money for the purchase of an ancient pueblo ruin by the Archeological Conservancy, and we were working on the sale with her. After not hearing from her for several days and being unable to contact her by phone, Lucia and I went to her house and found her passed away, lying peacefully in her bed.

She wanted to be buried in the national forest she had fought to protect over the years, but it is illegal. So as an alternative her friends got permission for her to be buried beneath a piñon tree in a small, old cemetery near El Morro Monument. Years before she had asked Dorn to build her casket when she died, and he did. As she requested, she was buried in her hiking clothes and sleeping bag.

Katherine was a fierce woman, beloved for the passion of her commitments, but someone with whom you didn't want to get crosswise. The casket Dorn made for her was beautiful and heavy and very securely fastened shut. When I asked him later why he sealed it with so many screws, he jokingly said, "She was tougher than a boot, and I wanted to make sure she stays put."

When Ken, who built our house, was killed in a collision with a gravel truck as he was driving back from Gallup, his wife, Doreen, asked Dorn to make a wooden box to hold his ashes. At Ken's ceremony the box sat on a pedestal under tall ponderosas in a grassy field across from their house. Mario and his wife, a Mexican couple who lived in the area, sang Mexican songs, and another friend played the flute.

Some days after the ceremony, Doreen got a friend to take her up a dirt road that trailed to the top of the mesa above her house. Her cousin held her feet as she leaned out over the edge of a massive stone promontory and scattered Ken's ashes into the gusty winds.

Dorn died several years later and because he died slowly, he could make his own casket. He was buried in it beneath a stone monument, also of his own making. Before the burial we held a send-off for him with barbecue, beer, music, and a passel of people, happy because they knew him and sad because he was gone.

We sent off several friends and neighbors during our twenty years in the area, and they were kindly cared for before their death. Folks made sure they always had food and a way to get to medical appointments in Gallup or Albuquerque, and visitors came by every day. Sometimes we struggled to get on the list to visit or provide transportation because so many people had already signed up. And when someone passed, they often had an intimate and unique celebration.

I don't know why death receives different treatment in Ramah compared to other places I've lived. Maybe it's a small-town thing, or maybe it's the nature of the people, who seem so sharply defined and open-hearted. Given my druthers, though, I'd rather pass away in a place like that.

As I ponder the regrets I have about the passing of various people in my life, I take comfort in something I once heard from a poet. In December 2019 we attended a gathering at the KiMo Theatre in Albuquerque to listen to Joy Harjo. Like Bear Heart, she is a member of the Muskogee Creek Nation. Harjo had just been named poet laureate, the first Native American to hold that position, and she talked about her life and recited from her latest book, *An American Sunrise*.

One of her most touching stories described how, after the death of her mother, she had wanted to wash her mother's body. However, the people from the mortuary arrived too soon and she had to allow them to take her mother away. One wonderful thing about poetry, though, Harjo said, is that it allows you to recreate past events as you wish they had gone. So, with the poem "Washing My Mother's Body," she went back in time and gave her mother the care she had yearned to provide.

13. Vampire Bugs

ALTHOUGH EACH PIECE OF the web of life is important to the whole, there are some creatures we could really do without, and in the Ramah area this proves particularly true of one tiny, biting bug. Some call them gnats, some call them no-see-ums, and some call them #X@%s, but everybody hates them. These nasty, little beasts come out in early summer to whine, bite, and leave angry welts that itch for days. Their proper name is cedar gnats, one of the thousands of species of biting midges that exist worldwide.

They lay their eggs in the fissures of cedar bark and after they hatch the larvae crawl around in the bark until fall, eating plant debris. Then they overwinter in the fissures and in June transform into a flying scourge that makes life miserable during the daylight hours for humans, cattle, horses, and other vertebrates.

Cedar gnats appear early to mid-June and usually disappear by the Fourth of July. In some years there are almost none, and many people say that a good rain will end their reign of terror. They won't bother before nine or so in the morning and don't come out after dusk. They love to bite in tight places, such as around the tops of socks and under belts, and they also gravitate toward hairlines. The insides of ears are especially delectable, so despite their sartorial shortcomings, mosquito net hats are a good idea. At least the gnats don't come inside houses, bite when people move quickly, or fly about when it's windy. They are weak fliers and generally don't go far from their hatching tree.

Male cedar gnats are innocent little things, beneficial in their way, mostly just eating nectar and pollinating flowers like bees, hummingbirds, and butterflies. But the females, like female mosquitoes, turn to the dark side when they mature and drink blood to get the protein they need to make eggs. They use their mandibles to gnaw a hole in the skin, spit anticoagulant in the wound, and suck up the pooling blood. And here's a line that could have come from one of Anne Rice's vampire books: Mating often occurs at the site of a blood host, shortly after the female has fed.

Consider this creepy image: A person is out in the garden pulling weeds when they hear a high, annoying whine, and soon a series of red welts begin to appear on their skin. They know immediately what's happening—a group of almost invisible vampire bugs have descended upon them to chew holes in their skin, feed on their blood, then engage in an orgy in the cedar trees that will result in more blood feasts to come the following year.

The gnats usually don't do lasting damage to humans, but they can seriously hurt cattle, horses, and wild animals by transmitting several pathogens to which the animals are vulnerable. Grazing animals, for instance, can be infected by a disease called bluetongue. Horses also sometimes suffer an allergic reaction to cedar gnats' anticoagulant and get a condition known as "sweet itch," which can result in severe skin irritation and hair loss.

Commercial repellants containing DEET are ineffective, but some products do hold them at bay. Avon's Skin So Soft may help, and some local folks make and sell homemade repellants that will do the job. We also find comfort in knowing that although the insects may plague us for a month or two, many locales have biting bugs throughout the warm season and sometimes even throughout the year.

Gnats aside, the Ramah area features other more fearsome small critters. In early fall we would notice large, hairy spiders ambling through the underbrush and taking perilous walks across highways. They were tarantulas, and though they looked scary, we knew they were basically harmless to humans. Slow walkers with a distinctive orange spot, they are reclusive, nocturnal, and reluctant to bite. If somehow one does bite you, it will hurt less than a bee sting. They usually remain close to their burrows, where they hunt for insects and small animals to eat. They do not spin webs, and the females can live up to thirty years.

Some folks keep tarantulas as pets, but they definitely have their unsettling side. Like all spiders they have eight separate eyes, two in the center of their face and six around them. They also inject their prey with venom to liquefy their innards so they can suck them empty. Finally, if a tarantula feels threatened, it can rub its legs against its abdomen and shoot hairs to cause chemical and physical damage to skin and mucous membranes.

Female tarantulas are giants of the spider world, but the males are only about a third their size and lead pitiful lives. The poor guys rarely live beyond ten years of age, and many get squashed on roads and highways in September when they go on walkabouts in search of the burrows of females. If they do find one and are lucky, they will mate and then die within a few weeks. If bad luck is their lot, they will come across a female who would rather eat them than have their babies.

So, when you see male tarantulas wandering through the ends of their short and brutish lives, wish them well. They might make your skin crawl a little, but they are nothing compared to their nemesis, the gigantic wasp known as the tarantula hawk. The tarantula hawk will capture and paralyze a tarantula with its stinger, drag it into its underground lair, then lay a single egg inside the spider's body. When the egg hatches, the wasp larva slowly eats the paralyzed but still living tarantula's body, consuming the vital heart and nervous system last.

14. Pueblo Indians

IN THE 1500S, WHEN the conquistadores encountered groups of Indians that lived in multistory adobe houses, they referred to them as "pueblos," the Spanish word for towns, and that is how they are known today. New Mexico is home to nineteen of the twenty-one pueblo tribes recognized by the federal government. The Hopi Tribe in Arizona and Ysleta del Sur in Texas are the only two outside of the state.

Unlike many other American Indian tribes who were forced by the US government to relocate, most pueblo communities remained on their ancestral land. They still inhabit areas where their forebears lived for millennia. Consequently, pueblo villages have a strong presence. Their ancient history, the long continuity of their culture, and their cruel treatment by the Spanish and American governments generate a sense of place that may be palpable to the sensitive visitor.

The Zuni Pueblo is a good example of this. The town of Zuni might well be the longest continually inhabited community in the United States (although two other pueblos, Acoma and Hopi, also claim this distinction). With nineteen thousand people, Zuni is the most populous pueblo in New Mexico, but only about six thousand tribal members live in the town of Zuni itself. Most live elsewhere on the reservation, which covers almost a thousand square miles.

Twelve miles from the town of Zuni are the ruins of Hawikuh, the ancient Zuni habitation that Coronado conquered in 1540 when he mistakenly believed it to be one of the legendary seven cities of gold. The conquest of Hawikuh marked the beginning of the Spanish colonization and suppression of the pueblos, for whom the reign was suppressive and severe. Puebloans suffered slavery, forced conversion to Christianity, and the banning of their own cultural and religious practices, which eventually led a San Juan Pueblo Native named Popé, along with leaders of other pueblos, to plan a revolution.

Popé realized that to be successful all the pueblos had to strike the Spaniards at the same time, so he sent runners to give each pueblo a knotted cord, with each knot representing one of the days left between the day they received the rope and the planned day of the uprising. Every day each pueblo would untie a knot until all the knots were gone, indicating the time had come for them all to rise up together.

The rebellion began on August 11, 1680, and it ultimately drove the Spanish out of what is today the state of New Mexico. Afterward, Popé and his lieutenants tried to return the pueblos to their old ways, ordering the destruction of Catholic churches, imported grain crops, and other things that smacked of their oppressors. Perhaps because of a lack of traditional coordination among the pueblos, Popé's dream of a unified Pueblo People soon died, and Popé himself died just before the somewhat more tolerant but still oppressive Spanish returned twelve years later.

Although today's pueblos share similar characteristics, they also differ in many ways. The Hopi, for instance, are considered by some to be the most culturally conservative of the pueblo people. They live primarily in small villages on the tops of three mesas on their reservation in northeastern Arizona and zealously guard the ceremonies and religious practices that guide much of their daily lives.

They welcome visitors, but always with the caveat that most of their sacred ceremonies and places are off limits.

Their secrecy flows in part from their belief that maintaining the purity of their religious practices is essential to the well-being of the entire earth. Also, like most traditional Indigenous peoples, they do not tolerate outsiders who misunderstand and misreport their ceremonies, especially when they see the Hopi as primitive or barbaric. Our visits to the Hopi Pueblo were always tinged with a high lonesome feel and a whiff of monastic mystery.

Acoma Pueblo also has a foundation of vital social tradition. The old town of Acoma sits atop a sheer-sided mesa sixty miles west of Albuquerque. On the edge of the mesa is an ancient cemetery surrounded by an adobe wall perforated with several holes. A tourist guide told us the holes allow the spirits of children enslaved and taken away by the Spanish to return home when they die.

Beside the cemetery stands a large, brown adobe mission, constructed in the early 1600s by the forced labor of Acoma men. Because the area has few trees, the wooden beams for the church had to be cut and transported on their backs from the San Mateo Mountains near Mount Taylor, thirty miles away. The conquistador Juan de Oñate was particularly brutal to Acoma; he put down a revolt at the pueblo in 1598 by killing hundreds of Acoma people and punishing all men twenty-five years of age or older by amputating one of their feet.

Like many cultures, that of Acoma contains a flood story. According to the tale, one day, when most people were working in the fields, a woman and her granddaughter were on the mesa top. A terrific storm arose and the mesa became surrounded by floodwaters. Eventually the food and water on the mesa ran out, and the woman and child held hands and leaped into the water. Rather than drowning they turned into butterflies, and it is said that their spirits are the source of the butterflies still abundant up there.

Another New Mexico pueblo, Laguna, celebrates the feast day of their patron saint, St. Joseph, on March 19, and outsiders are welcome to partake. Katherine, who had worked as a nurse for the pueblo, took us there one year, and we attended a Catholic Mass strongly blended with Laguna tradition. The priest spoke in Keres, the Laguna language, and in addition to his Catholic liturgical vestments, he wore a Laguna necklace and a pair of moccasins. The Mass took place in their picturesque, whitewashed mission, which sits on a hill above the village, and it included speeches by elder tribal men, one of whom held a silver-headed cane that President Lincoln presented to the pueblo in 1863. Lincoln gave canes to each New Mexico pueblo that year, in acknowledgment of their sovereignty. A group of elder tribal women also participated, chanting and dancing in place.

After Mass a procession of Laguna people carrying a carved figure of St. Joseph wound through the streets and old adobe buildings. It eventually ended in the central plaza, where a drumming circle that included the Catholic priest pounded out a rhythmic cadence beneath a bower of fresh evergreen branches. A harvest dance was performed by women and girls who all wore white gloves, possibly a Spanish addition to their much older traditional garb.

Taos Pueblo, adjacent to Taos, New Mexico, is a picturesque community that also carries a fascinating history. Its ancient adobe structures are adjacent to the Pueblo de Taos River, a small stream that originates in the Sangre de Cristo Mountains and runs free and clear because its upper reaches flow through protected pueblo land.

We have visited Taos Pueblo several times, though when we tried to visit one February we couldn't enter because the pueblo always closes that month to cleanse its energy. The entrance to the pueblo is about two blocks from a gas station on the edge of town, and if you are receptive, you may be startled to feel the shift that happens in those two blocks between the modern town to the pueblo so anchored in deep tradition. Taos Pueblo has existed for over a thousand years and was visited by a detachment from Coronado's expedition in 1540, the same year Coronado's main force conquered the Zuni town of Hawikuh.

Within the pueblo are the ruins of a Catholic church, where, during the Mexican American War, a group of Hispanic New Mexicans and Taos Indians who opposed American takeover of the territory took refuge in 1847. Because American cannons couldn't penetrate the thick adobe walls, they set the church roof on fire, and most of the people inside burned to death. The ruins remain as a memorial of the tragic event.

The rebels responsible for the Taos Revolt were angered by repressive actions of the US Army and feared that the American government would not respect their land titles originally issued by the Mexican government. The rebellion was quickly quelled, and the Guadalupe Hildalgo Treaty that formally ended the Mexican American War in 1848 affirmed the property rights of New Mexico's Hispanic and Native residents.

Although I only touch upon Zuni, Hopi, Acoma, Laguna, and Taos, the five pueblos with which we are most familiar, all pueblos are steeped in tradition, mystery, and painful history. Puebloans, like other Native peoples in New Mexico, still carry collective wounds from their mistreatment by the Spanish. They find particular offense in New Mexico's ubiquitous statues of their conquistador oppressors, especially those of Juan de Oñate. During the Black Lives Matter protests in 2020, when confederate monuments were removed from many places in this country, similar demonstrations in New Mexico demanded the removal of monuments dedicated to Spanish conquistadores, and some were destroyed by the protestors themselves.

The countryside where we lived contains many reminders of the ancestors of today's pueblo communities. In the past those early people were referred to as "Anasazi," but this word is derived from a Navajo word meaning "ancient enemies" and is no longer considered appropriate. Today they are called "Ancestral Puebloans," and they existed in northern New Mexico most densely for the hundred years between AD 1275 and 1375. After that period most of them gradually relocated to lower elevations, including the places currently occupied by their descendants. On our walks around the Ramah area we sometimes encountered Ancestral Puebloan ruins and their grinding tools, projectile points, and other artifacts.

When I came across a sherd from an Ancestral Pueblo pot, I sometimes thought about the people who formed and decorated it and used it ceremonially or in their daily lives. Imagine the durability of those fragments made of painted and fired clay, retaining their shapes and colors through hundreds of summers and winters and looking almost as they did on the day they broke off from their pots so long ago.

Ancestral Puebloans also inhabited the magnificent dwellings in northwestern New Mexico at Chaco Canyon. Chaco was a central location from which the Ancestral Puebloan system of towns and commerce extended outward for hundreds of miles. Compared to the ruins at Chaco Canyon, the settlements in the Ramah area are much smaller and simpler, inhabited by rural folks who subsisted on deer, rabbits, and wild plants, and grew corn and beans and squash (sometimes referred to as the three sisters). Archaeologists tell us that the small ruin still visible in the cliff face beside Timberlake Road, the road that led to our house, was a granary—an enclosure used to store corn.

No one knows exactly why Chaco and other prominent Ancestral Puebloan communities were eventually depopulated. There are many theories, but those most often suggested blame drought and attacks by other Indian groups. We do know, however, that the Ancestral Puebloans were not the first humans who inhabited the area where we lived; other people arrived thousands of years before them. Nor, of course, were they the last. After the Ancestral Puebloans came today's Puebloans, and later the Navajo, Apache, and other tribes; then came the Spaniards and Mexicans, and all the rest of us. All those people and cultures, stacked and blended for thousands of years, constitute the rich human mélange that makes New Mexico the fascinating mosaic it is today.

15. The Navajo Nation

IN THE RAMAH AREA we had more contact with the Navajo than any other tribal group, in large part because they were among our closest neighbors. The Ramah Navajo Reservation, a noncontiguous part of the large Navajo Reservation, sits just a few miles away. We had Navajo friends, and members of the tribe helped build our house and repair it. They, like the Zuni, fought wildfires in our area, and their tribal police patrolled our roads, which provided vital augmentation to our scarce county resources.

The Navajo Nation is the largest reservation in the country, greater in area than ten of the fifty states. About the size of West Virginia, it extends more than twenty-seven thousand square miles across New Mexico, Arizona, and Utah. In 2021, with four hundred thousand members, they also became the most populous tribe in the US, edging out the Cherokee.

Navajos often refer to themselves as Diné, the word in their language that means "the people." The Tribal Council has twice considered legislation that would change the name of the tribe from the Navajo Nation to the Diné Nation and rejected the idea both times on the basis that it would create frustration and confusion. Tribal members use both terms, which I will do as well.

Ancestors of the Diné and the Apache migrated at roughly the same time from Canada and Alaska to what is now the Southwest United States. Both tribes speak Athabaskan languages (a family of North American Native languages) that are similar enough for some people to consider them variants of the same tongue. The two will sometimes kid each other, Navajo saying Apache speak the language too fast, and Apache claiming Navajo speak it too slow. Because both languages are closely related to those of some Alaskan and Canadian tribes, Navajo and Apache can, to some extent, speak directly with those people as well.

Broad generalizations about Native people are almost always oversimplifications. Native Americans are no more contained in separate boxes than anyone else. Their ancestry is often a mix of ethnicities. A Hopi group, for instance, referred to as the Hopi Tewa, consists of descendants of people who fled to Hopi from other pueblo tribes during the Pueblo Revolt of 1680. Also, many Diné believe that some Navajo clans were established long ago by Pueblo women who had become Navajo.

We often encountered people whose parents descended from different tribes, and, of course, countless individuals in the general population have Native ancestry in their lineage. Probably the most common criterion used by Native tribes to determine membership is blood quantum, the percentage of an individual's ancestry in that tribe.

Some years ago we attended an exhibit at the Navajo Nation Museum in the town of Window Rock, the capital of the Navajo Nation. Window Rock sits just across the Arizona border from New Mexico, and the museum has an excellent collection of Navajo art. The show we saw displayed examples of Diné artistry side by side with Tibetan work, and the similarities were uncanny.

From silver and turquoise jewelry to woven rugs to pottery, the designs and color patterns were so alike that without labels the untutored eye could not tell from which culture each artwork came.

It was a striking demonstration of the commonality between the Diné and the Tibetan people in Asia, the continent from where Diné ancestors migrated. And those migrations were fairly recent when compared to the ancestors of the Puebloans, who migrated here thousands of years ago. The Navajo ancestors came to the Southwest just two or three hundred years before the Spanish arrived.

The relative recency of the Diné in the area is one of the reasons their towns have such a different energy than those of pueblo tribes. Many Navajo communities look and feel much like other small towns in America, while Pueblo villages, often containing ancient adobe structures, seem steeped in generations of communal ceremonies and traditions.

Also, many Diné live in extended family groups scattered throughout the countryside. Navajo ancestors were not town dwellers; they were nomadic hunter-gatherers. Puebloan ancestors, on the other hand, tended to be farmers, and their settlements reflect their agricultural need for sedentary living, at least during the growing season, and their requirement for places where food and seed can be stored and protected.

The cultures of both groups, though, are ancient and complex. Navajo spiritual and religious practices have an underlying focus on maintaining balance and harmony within the individual, the community, and the natural world, as reflected in the phrase often associated with them, "Walk in Beauty." As N. Scott Momaday said in the preface to his Pulitzer Prize–winning novel, *House Made of Dawn*, the Navajo people carry "a culture that is ancient, noble, and deeply informed with aesthetic and spiritual principles."

Many of the products Navajo offer to tourists are based on their spiritual traditions. When visitors purchase sand paintings, for instance, they are buying reflections of sacred images created by Navajo medicine people for use in medicine practices. The images are made from colored sand and get erased after those involved in the ceremony sit or lie upon them. In this they resemble Tibetan

Buddhist sand mandalas that are destroyed soon after being created. Also, Yeibichai figures often portrayed on Navajo rugs are portraits of dancers and medicine people dressed as they might be for the Night Chant, the first performance in a nine-day religious and healing ceremony.

As with many traditional cultural practices, Diné medicine coexists with the medicine of physicians and hospitals. For example, we became friends with a modern Navajo family, and one day the father, Anthony, told us about a serious illness of his father who was receiving all the help Western medicine could provide. He also described the medicine ceremony his community held for his father, which lasted several days under the direction of a Diné medicine man.

The Diné, like most Indigenous people in this country, suffered grievously at the hands of the United States government. One of the most infamous occurrences was the Trail of Tears, which they remember as their Long Walk. During several months in 1864 some nine thousand Navajo men, women, and children were forced to walk over three hundred miles from their land in Arizona to internment at a desolate reservation called Bosque Redondo in eastern New Mexico.

Through blistering summer and frigid winter, old and young and in-between trudged with inadequate clothing and little help from the US Army. Many died along the way, perishing in childbirth, drowning in the Rio Grande, or being shot as stragglers. Of those who survived, about a third died later because of the terrible conditions of starvation and neglect at Bosque Redondo. In 1868 the "relocation experiment" was abandoned and the Navajo were allowed to return to a small reservation created by the US government in their Arizona homeland.

Despite, and perhaps to some extent because of, the harsh treatment of Indigenous people by this country, more American Indians have served in the US Armed Forces per capita than any other ethnic group. In addition to being warriors, they performed a unique encryption service during World War II. By transmitting information over radios in their tribal languages, they provided communication that our enemies could not decode. They were called code talkers, and they came from several tribes.

Particularly well known were the four hundred Navajos recruited to serve in that capacity with the marines in the Pacific theater. After the war, Navajo code talkers were celebrated as heroes for the rest of their lives. They were honored at powwows and Memorial Day celebrations where they told stories, gave autographs, and were photographed. The last Navajo code talker, Chester Nez, died on June 4, 2014, at the age of ninety-three.

Like that of many groups in the Southwest, the Navajo story is interwoven with the histories of others. This holds especially true regarding the Canyon de Chelly National Monument on the Navajo Reservation just across the New Mexico border in northeastern Arizona. Both Navajo and Hopi revere the canyon, which is steeped in a richness of Ancient Puebloan habitation.

Canyon de Chelly is also a good example of a productive partnership between a tribe and the federal government. Ownership of the land rests with the Navajo Tribal Trust, and the tribe and the National Park Service share management responsibility.

Visitors can travel the canyon floor with a Diné guide or drive themselves along the canyon rims and stop at lookouts where views include the White House Ancestral Puebloan cliff dwellings, Spider Rock, which ascends 750 feet from the canyon floor, and meandering streams and green trees and foliage far below. A few Diné families live and farm in the bottom of the canyon in the summer and move to the canyon's rim for winter.

Canyon de Chelly contains some 2,700 archeological sites and has seen human habitation for about 5,000 years. The last battle between the Navajo and federal troops, led by Kit Carson, also occurred here in 1863. This conflict marked the end of significant

Navajo resistance, just a year before their infamous Long Walk. The rich mix of natural beauty, Native cultures, and tragic history give the area a strong sense of place.

The Navajo hogans, traditional Diné structures usually made of wooden planks or logs, remain a persistent memory of the area for me. A majority of those we saw were rounded with six or eight sides, no windows, and a door opening to the east to welcome the rising sun. They are called female hogans and can be used as homes. The less common male hogans are taller, circular structures with much smaller interiors and are usually used for ceremonial purposes.

Lucia and I particularly remember a hogan we came across when visiting Canyon de Chelly with our friend Deborah, on a day of constantly changing weather. As we explored along the canyon rim, the bright sky clouded and a high wind began to blow, filling the air with dust. Then it rained and changed to snow, and soon after the blue sky returned. During the snowy period we came across a hogan that contained a small store.

We parked and walked through the blowing snow, and when we entered we found ourselves in a warm space with a dirt floor and a wood stove. A few tables and shelves held handicrafts and souvenirs, and a Diné couple offered welcoming smiles and greetings. We lingered, chatted, and left, grateful for having experienced how very comforting, especially as a haven from blowing snow, the traditional Navajo structure can be.

16. Starry, Starry Night

SITTING ON THE FLAT roof of our house beneath a clear night sky, Lucia and I saw something that, because of air pollution and light from cities, most people on earth will never see. The sky was resplendent with the dense, bright smear of the Milky Way and clusters of other stars everywhere.

Occasional airplanes and satellites, high and silent, moved slowly across the vault from west to east and east to west. Perhaps because it is a binary or double star, Sirius flashed red and green and blue, and even between regular meteor showers we often glimpsed a shooting star. Our gaze would drift among stars scattered along the tops of sandstone cliffs and catch their twinkling through the pines.

Seeking patterns in the bright vertigo, we spotted the Big Dipper, the northern pole star, and Orion's Belt, then we slipped down into our house where pools of yellow light transitioned us to the cozy warmth of our inside world, though the night remained with us. Our bed lay beneath a skylight that framed a rectangle of stars, and a bank of tall windows in the curved bedroom wall flooded the room with moon and starlight. As we dozed off, our dog, Walter, slept on his bed beside the windows, awash in it all.

Sometimes after returning home at night and pulling into our garage, we would step out under the sky and one of us would whisper, "Look at that!" People where we lived tended to talk in hushed voices when out beneath the stars, nightly reminders of the vastness of which we are a part. Perhaps awe of the night sky is even embedded in our DNA, a connection to the universal mystery experienced throughout our long evolutionary path.

The visibility of the stars out there made it easy to imagine how our distant ancestors relied on the patterns of the night sky, and ancient ruins are replete with examples. In the Peruvian complex of Machu Picchu, for example, the Pisac Sun Temple sits atop a massive stack of terraces. Within the temple a stone marks the arrival of the winter solstice when the sun illuminates one side of it, and when the sun lights the stone's other side, the summer solstice has come. Machu Picchu also contains other indicators of the celestial calendar that allowed important activities, such as planting, harvesting, and holding ceremonies, to occur at their proper times.

In our part of the world Chaco Culture National Historical Park in northwestern New Mexico contains the ruins of a great and intricate cultural center of the Ancestral Puebloans. The perfectly fitted stone structures in Chaco were the largest buildings in North America until the nineteenth century, and many of them align with the cycles of the sun and moon. The best-known astronomical indicator there is the sun dagger petroglyph panel atop Fajada Butte, where three vertical sandstone slabs focus sunlight onto the big spiral petroglyph during the solstices. The panel also contains a glyph that marks the equinoxes.

We don't have to look back to ancient civilizations, though, to find Indigenous spiritual connections to the night sky; it is imbued in the cultures of many Native groups today. The Navajo, for instance, have an entire system of astronomy based on their own complex set of constellations oriented to the locations of their four sacred mountains. Each celestial element has cultural import, reflecting the Navajo relationship to the rest of the universe. As an example, Polaris, the pole star, represents the fire in the center of the hogan. The hogan, like the pole star, is an unmoving anchor around which everything else rotates.

Nancy C. Maryboy, president and founder of the Indigenous Education Institute, authored a collection of curricula to accompany a planetarium demonstration of Navajo astronomy, which contains an excellent description of the Diné relationship to the cosmos. I offer a portion of it here as an example of a traditional star-based Indigenous philosophy:

> The Navajo worldview includes a holistic and ordered universe where everything is interrelated and all the pieces of the universe are enfolded within the whole. At the same time, every piece contains the entire universe, creating a network of relationships and processes in constant flux. Unlike Western astronomy, traditional Navajo astronomy is highly spiritual in accordance with a worldview where everything is considered living and sacred. The entire universe is considered to be a living organism, a sacred organism existing in a non-static and constantly regenerating process. The human is an integral participant within the dynamic whole.

———————

The Hopi's belief system also relates to the night sky. In their cosmology the creator made nine worlds, seven to be inhabited by beings other than gods. Humans inhabited the first three, which were each destroyed in turn because the people became corrupt. We now reside in the fourth world, which will also be destroyed for the same reason when the Blue Star Kachina appears in the sky. Those Hopi who have maintained the integrity of their lives and their faith, however, will be taken underground, protected, and then returned to populate the purified fifth world.

A Zuni children's story relating to the night sky sometimes came to mind when we saw insects called darkling beetles. If you bother or touch a darkling beetle, it tilts forward so its head is near the earth and its rear is in the air. This is a warning that it will spray whatever threatens them with a smelly liquid. According to the Zuni tale, darkling beetles were given the honor of carrying sacks of stars into the night sky and placing each where it belonged. All the beetles performed their tasks properly except one, who tripped and spilled all the stars out of his sack. This formed the Milky Way and also explains why darkling beetles tip forward and bow their heads, shamed by their ancestor's clumsy mistake.

Today, because of human activity, the night sky continues to dim, but glimmers of hope remain. When sooner or later the climate crisis forces us to reduce air pollution, a peripheral benefit will be brighter stars. Also, we are beginning to enact laws to control light pollution. The state of New Mexico, for instance, recognized the human, scientific, and tourist value of the night sky by enacting in 1999 the New Mexico Night Sky Protection Act that regulates outdoor lighting.

The New Mexico Tourism Department also acknowledged the value of our clear skies by creating the New Mexico True Dark Skies Trail. The trail includes the six state and national parks and monuments in New Mexico that the International Dark Sky Association has designated as international dark skies parks, one of which is the Chaco Culture National Historic Park. El Morro National Monument, in our old neighborhood, is another dark skies park. The skies there are so bright and clear that a private observatory just off Highway 53 near the monument provides astronomical observations to scientists and universities around the world. In 2017 *Travel and Leisure Magazine* named New Mexico one of the world's top ten stargazing spots, a perfect place for astrotourism.

A couple of years ago Matt, his wife, Eed, and their sons, Kenny and Nate, spent Christmas with us. It was a typical high-country wintertime with crystal clear night skies. A few days after Christmas

Kenny was sending applications to colleges and had one more application to transmit over the Internet. As he was about to push the button on his laptop, Matt said, "Why don't we all go up on the roof and send it from there?"

And so we did. We bundled up, got a flashlight, turned off the lights in the house so the only light would be from the stars, and crunched through the snow and up the stairs to the roof. As he settled into the cold, Kenny turned on his computer and hunched over the screen. The rest of us held hands and counted to three, and Kenny pushed the button to fire his application into the canopy above our heads.

We could almost see the message streak through the stars and arc over the earth, to a computer at a university on the other side of the country. It felt like magic—this small circle of family on the roof of a remote house in the frozen winter night, sending a request through the universe shining above us.

We are literally children of the stars; every atom in our bodies was created in the furnaces of stars that died long ago. As the astronomer Carl Sagan once put it, "We are a way for the universe to know itself. Some part of our being knows this is where we come from. We long to return. And we can, because the cosmos is also within us." We are, however, in danger of losing that knowing, as our visibility of the night sky dims. To me this is a very sad possibility, perhaps even a subtle limitation of our ability to be a global tribe together. Gazing at the stars gives us all common ground and connects us to the vastness of creation.

As the globe perilously warms, we need that perspective. If humans are to survive, we must see ourselves in the Indigenous way, as part of a natural system that must be respected and preserved. There are movements in that direction; many scientists and government officials are taking up the call to change the way we live so the earth can return to balance, and we are listening better to the wisdom of our often forgotten and disrespected Native people, as more and more of them assume positions of leadership in the wider culture.

New Mexico, for example, elected two Native women to the US House of Representatives in recent years, and one of them, Deb Haaland, a member of Laguna Pueblo, was named Secretary of the Interior, where she became a strong and capable champion for climate crisis solutions, preservation of natural resources, and Native rights. In addition, Kathryn Iso-Clause, a member of Taos Pueblo, became the Department of Interior Assistant Secretary for Indian Affairs, an appointment with great practical and symbolic significance for Native sovereignty.

In addition to observing the starry sky from earth, there is another way to enhance our global relationship: gazing down from space upon our world. The picture captured by the crew of the Apollo 17 spacecraft on December 7, 1972, called the "Blue Marble photo," is one of the most iconic ever taken. For many people, seeing our tiny, fragile globe, with its paper-thin layer of atmosphere as it floats in the black infinity of space, ignited a visceral understanding of it as Gaia, a precious living entity that should be nourished and protected.

Even more powerfully, many astronauts are so deeply affected when they directly see the earth from space that they experience a fundamental shift in their value system and worldview. The phenomenon is called the "overview effect," a term coined by philosopher Frank White, who wrote a book about it in 1987. It may be among the most significant legacies of our ventures into space.

Astronauts have described the overview effect as rushes of emotional appreciation for our need to protect the earth and cease warring against each other. Astronaut Edgar Mitchell said, "You develop an instant global consciousness, a people orientation, an intense dissatisfaction with the state of the world and a compulsion to do something about it." In 2022 the actor William Shatner was so profoundly impacted by seeing the earth from space that he wept as he said, "What I would love to do is to communicate as much as possible the jeopardy, the moment you see the vulnerability of everything. This air which is keeping us alive is thinner than your skin."

As awareness of the overview effect has grown, it has borne a movement to replicate the experience for the general population through writing, video, and virtual reality. Two overview effects institutes have been established, one in the United States and the other in Australia. Some believe that the overview effect could become a primary pathway to developing a worldwide consciousness of the need for world peace and unity, an inoculant for the protection of the earth and all its inhabitants.

Finally, in, of all places, the field of law, a very promising blossom has arisen. An article in *Wired Magazine* described a surprising and heartening trend of enacting statutes that grant personhood to nature. The city of Toledo, Ohio, for instance, passed an ordinance in 2019 to give legal rights to Lake Erie, so city residents can file lawsuits on behalf of the lake to enforce its right to freedom from pollution. A river in New Zealand and an area in the country of Colombia have also been given legal rights. The article's author, Clive Thompson, reports that:

> Environmentalists have prodded governments and courts to award rights to lakes, hills, rivers, and even individual species of plants. . . . About three dozen towns across the US are passing Toledo-style bills, and the Florida Democratic Party lists the rights of nature in its party platform. . . . Indigenous groups have been at the forefront of this legal movement. . . . In 2018 the White Earth Band of the Chippewa Tribe in Minnesota gave legal rights to wild rice in their tribal courts. . . . If we're going to rein in our abuse of nature, we need to see it as our equal.

Hopefully, we will continue to extend, by law and intent, environmental quality rights to each other and the living earth itself, and maybe even begin to see the stars clearly once more.

17. Medicine Wheel and a Blessing

SHORTLY AFTER WE HAD moved in to our new home, a painter doing touch-ups asked us if we were interested in landscaping the yard around the house. "There's a woman named Mary Anne," he said, "who lived all last winter in a teepee. She's a trained landscaper and would probably like the work."

"Perhaps at some point," we replied. Although the area between the adobe wall around our yard and the house was just a flat expanse of hard-packed clay, we didn't feel like we could take on another project just then.

The concept of a modern woman living alone in a teepee through the long, often bitter-cold winter weather intrigued us, and we knew that a great deal of the magic and artistry of our house existed because of our openness to and gratitude for the creative gifts of the people who joined in the process of the home's making. We kept thinking about Mary Anne and finally decided to reach out. Because she still lived in the teepee without electricity or running water, much less a phone, we couldn't call her directly, but we eventually got a meeting set up and quickly took to each other.

Mary Anne was a soft-spoken woman in her early forties with an encyclopedic knowledge of plants. She loved growing things and working with soil and stone and bringing everything together to create beautiful spaces. She itched to get her hands on the blank canvas of our yard, and we were eager to get it into her hands, so we agreed on a price that was more than we thought we could spend and less than the work deserved.

The next time Mary Anne came over a handsome young Navajo man named Jones accompanied her. As we got to know him we learned that he experienced a long mix of family difficulties, but he had an artist's heart and a boyish face that lit up with pleasure when he created. He enjoyed working in the earth and had a particular talent with stones.

The ground around our house was so compacted by the building process that I couldn't drive a spike into it with a hammer, so Mary Anne and Jones began by breaking up the soil with pickaxes. Then they added soil amendments, including composted sheep manure that was readily available to them on Navajo land. We could not believe the work the two of them put into creating good soil before they even began laying out beds and walks. By the time they finished our feet sank into the soft loam.

Next came flagstone walks and flowerbeds. They hauled large and small lichen-covered rocks from high Navajo land in Mary Anne's old pickup truck and brought in other stones they thought would be right for the place. One came from a remote area where members of Jones's family had purportedly seen a UFO land.

With his mother's guidance Jones created a small medicine wheel with rocks, placed a rock seat at its center, and built another bench of rough stone beside the adobe wall that encircled the yard. Then he dug a hole in the middle of the patio, lined it with lava rock, and extended the stone sides fifteen inches above the ground. "Here," he said, "is your fire pit." Some of our most memorable occasions were evenings sitting with friends and family in lawn chairs around that pit, watching cedar and piñon coals glow in the dark.

Next, they moved on to plants. Most were from the general

area, and they collected each with reverence and a blessing, digging them out carefully to save as much root and soil as possible. They did not take a plant unless they could see seven more of the same species from the spot where the plant grew. Day after day, Mary Anne and Jones drove into the yard, their truck loaded down with rocks and plants. In went cactus and yucca, sage and desert rose. Then Mary Anne added bulbs and seeds she had brought from a visit to her family garden in Maryland. We added three locust trees and a few Russian sage bushes from a greenhouse in Gallup, and eventually the gift of their creativity surrounded our house.

One day in early September we went to Gallup to run some errands, leaving the two of them working in the yard. When we returned Mary Anne told us that we had missed a visitor. A tarantula had wandered through the yard and over the top of the wall, walking in their deliberate way like a cat in slow motion. She watched it amble and almost caught it for us to see, but decided it shouldn't be disturbed on its journey. In Kansas City the migration of ducks and geese marks the fall season. The Ramah area also had ducks and geese, but they weren't the most interesting harbingers of autumn—those were the male tarantulas on their love-seeking walkabouts.

We have a strong image of the two of them, Mary Anne barefoot and ankle-deep in dirt, muscled arms and shoulders moving and planting and caressing, and Jones, small of build but just as strong, bare to the waist and wielding a pickax. Occasionally they would work past sunset, and afterward we would build a fire in the fire pit and sit and talk. Over the three-month period it took to build our garden we became friends.

In late fall we had a dinner to celebrate the completion of their work. Mary Anne, Jones, and Jones's mother came, as did Mary Anne's brother Jay and his partner, Randy, who were visiting from Savannah. Mary Anne brought a big pot of pork and chocolate mole, Jones's mother made fry bread, and Lucia supplied all the other fixings and trimmings. Before dinner Jones offered a prayer in Navajo and passed around a glass of water so each person could sprinkle themselves and ask for a personal blessing.

After dinner we all went out into the cool, clear evening to sit around the fire pit and talk. Lucia suggested we each speak of what we were grateful for and surprisingly, even though we gathered to celebrate the completion of the garden, it was not much mentioned. Everyone spoke mostly of friendship and the gifts we had received from each other.

Jones expressed gratitude for meeting Lucia and me and, to my great surprise, for some aspects of the arrival of Europeans on this continent. I always assumed that for Native Americans the arrival of Europeans was about as happy an event as the arrival of the bubonic plague. But Jones talked about the gifts the Europeans brought, such as science and writing and law, necessary tools for Native Americans to move with the rest of the world into the future. I think to some extent he was being kind, trying to soften barriers between us, of resentment and guilt borne of the harsh treatment of his ancestors by ours.

Long after the garden's completion, Jones would show up once in a while to see if we had a little work for him and to talk. He had become a peacekeeper for his tribe, a trained volunteer who interceded in conflict to resolve anger. He attended an international conference of peacekeepers in Phoenix and saw the similarities of his efforts to those of others around the world. During one visit, he mentioned that two groups of Indians, consisting of Navajo and other tribal members, had gathered in the mountains in our area to stir up trouble. They had come to create anger and dissension, but Navajo medicine people were aware of their activities and planned to do what they could to counter them.

Over the following years we continued to care for and shape the garden. We weeded and watered and fertilized, added more flowers and bushes and trees, and had friends construct a tiny pond with water burbling over a few rocks. What began as a barren stretch of ground became a beloved part of our home, a place we inhabited as if it were another room.

A great deal of work went into maintaining the garden, but the work was strength-building and meditative. Many lizards inhabited our garden, and it always made me happy to see them watching me, as if they had become benevolent guardians of the place.

18. Fire and Ice

WE OFTEN SAT ON the patio of our house in the summer dusk, watching bats darting in and out of our garden, around the trees, and almost colliding with our faces. Those amazing navigators swerved and swooped so fast we struggled to follow them with our eyes and had fun trying not to flinch when they barely flared away. We never got hit—their echolocation operated flawlessly as they dodged among trees and people to catch insects in the fading light.

They were Mexican free-tailed bats, perhaps the most abundant mammals in North America and the fastest horizontal flyers, with a top speed of over one hundred miles per hour. Even though they were fairly small, we still got a thrill when they almost slammed into us.

In addition to being entertaining, bats eat massive amounts of flying insects, particularly mosquitos. Some people try to attract them to their yards by putting bat houses in their trees, but the Mexican free-tailed bats prefer to roost in caves where they can spend their days sleeping among thousands of their ilk. Carlsbad Caverns National Park in Carlsbad, New Mexico, is renowned for its enormous bat colonies, and thanks to extensive former volcanic activity, they graced our area as well.

Because New Mexico contains the largest number and diversity of volcanoes in North America, it could rightly be called the volcanic state. Young volcanoes are especially abundant here, some less than four thousand years old (a blink of an eye in geologic time). The young ones include those at El Malpais National Monument on Highway 53 and throughout the surrounding El Malpais National Conservation Area. El Malpais is Spanish for "the bad land," an apt description for country deeply covered in sharp-edged lava. The two areas together preserve almost four hundred thousand acres of lava fields and extinct volcanoes.

Common among El Malpais volcanoes are structures called lava tubes, created when molten lava forms thick ropes. Because the inside of the lava ropes remains hot and continues to flow after the outside has cooled and hardened, it leaves behind long, dark tunnels. Sometimes the tops of the tubes collapse, allowing bats access to roost inside in huge numbers.

El Malpais National Monument has a path to a lava tube that is a primary roost for bats, and we took an outing there one summer evening with friends and family. We packed up snacks and a bottle of wine, put the two smallest kids in a red wagon, and set out at about six-thirty in the evening. The waning day was cool at that altitude of 7,200 feet, and the sky was partly cloudy with a full moon. We arrived at the cave entrance, a large, jagged hole in the top of a lava tube, laid out our blankets, and settled in for the show, the only audience that evening.

Within about forty-five minutes we noticed a slight urine smell, and then a few bats flitted out of the hole in front of us. After a while the flight of bats became a large stream as thousands of them rushed out to begin their night of feeding. We sat there on a hillside close to the cave mouth, transfixed by the intensifying flow.

Eventually the flow slowed and stopped, and we began packing up to leave. Then someone in our group said, "Look," and we all turned to see the full yellow moon with a long, winding stream of bats across its face. It was a moment of magic reminiscent of the scene in the movie *The Wizard of Oz* when a wavering line of flying monkeys snakes across the moon's face.

The volcanic lava rock there is mostly vesicular basalt, full of holes that make it very light in weight and also sharp and abrasive. A walk over a lava-covered area requires care to avoid injury and can quickly tear apart a pair of tennis shoes. But the material is good for making stone grinding tools, which the Ancestral Puebloans did.

It's hard to walk cross-country very long in the Ramah area without encountering artifacts made by the Ancestral Puebloans, which on occasion include stone tools. Among them are the stone basins called metates that held corn or other plants or minerals to be ground, and manos (the Spanish word for hands), the implements used to do the grinding.

The manos could be small disks for use with one hand or flat, elongated stones for two-handed work, usually made of sandstone, granite, or vesicular basalt. Archeologists suggest that because of the holes, the vesicular basalt manos were probably used for the first coarse grind, followed by a finer grind with manos made of denser stone.

One day while out hiking I noticed the edge of a piece of vesicular basalt protruding from the ground. Because no volcanoes exist in the immediate area, I knew the stone must have been carried in and most probably was an Ancestral Puebloan tool. Sure enough, I pulled from the earth a lovely two-handed mano. I especially appreciate manos because I can almost sense the people who used them over and over to prepare their family's food. I like to imagine them in their hands and wonder if some small residue of skin or oil worked its way into the stones' pores, still there after centuries in the soil.

Counterintuitively, in addition to fire, ice can also form as a result of volcanos. Ice can be found in some deep lava tubes where, even in the hottest summers, it never melts. You can visit such a lava tube cave at the Ice Caves on Highway 53, between Ramah and El Malpais National Monument, which we did one hot summer day. As we descended the seventy steps into the tube, the air became cooler and cooler until we shivered at the bottom and peered into a small cavern of green and white ice on the cave floor and back wall.

The temperature at the cave bottom never gets above thirty-one degrees Fahrenheit, and the ice is some twenty feet thick. It is created by water that seeps in from the surface and freezes, then becomes preserved by the high insulation quality of the basalt. The green in some of the ice comes from a species of algae that can survive below-freezing temperatures. It is apparently nontoxic because Indians harvested the ice and ate it for centuries. The ice was also used in the thirties and forties to chill beer in the long-gone Ice Cave Trading Post Saloon that stood nearby.

The mounded calderas of dormant volcanoes are exotic parts of the landscape. Bats, ancient stone tools, and perennial ice are among the gifts we know they hold, but there must be, hidden among the sharp rocks and daunting fissures of the vast Malpais, a multitude of other treasures yet undiscovered.

19. Sense of Place

SENSE OF PLACE IS a phrase widely used and variously defined over the years. Some writers, such as Wallace Stegner and Wendell Berry, see it as something borne of a long and intimate relationship between a location and an individual. The sense of place I am talking about here is different, discernible even to a new visitor.

Much of New Mexico carries this sense of place strongly, and the Ramah area fairly exudes it. Taos, New Mexico, also has a strong sense of place, and folks say there that "the mountain either sucks you in or spits you out." In his book *West of the Thirties*, anthropologist and cross-cultural researcher Edward T. Hall expressed it this way: "In my experience, each country has a flavor all its own, a mystique unique to it and its people . . . The flavor of Hopi and Navajo country was almost palpable, and I began to catalog mentally the places I visited in terms of the feelings they evoked. I was discovering a new kind of geography."

In some places in the Ramah area the energy is more palpable than in others. I would occasionally explore a spot down Timberlake Road a mile or so from our house; I'd park beside the road, put on my hat, pick up my stick, and head up the hill. After hiking across a glen and up another hill, along a ridge and through the ponderosas and scrub oak, I'd come to a high, flat meadow. There, hundreds of years earlier, an Ancestral Puebloan group had lived in a few stone dwellings dug into the ground. Not much remained, just low lines of stone and jumbled rocks scattered about and some small mounds that marked digs of pot hunters years earlier. I'd poke about, looking under bushes and along dirt piles at occasional small pottery sherds, and wonder about those people from long ago and how they lived.

One late spring afternoon as I stood there musing, a voice in my head told me to sit down on one of the stone piles on the edge of the meadow. I did and glanced around, my awareness flitting from this small thought to that, until I sensed a voice in my mind saying, "Be still." I emptied my thoughts and let my eyes settle on the dappled sunlight below the hill. I don't know how long I sat there, but I was completely at peace, awash in the knowledge that everything, including myself, was just as it should be. Eventually the spell lifted, and I rose slowly and worked my way down to the road and home. I am not a New Age person, just a guy from Wichita, but I can still call upon the comfort of that experience. Before I left I picked up a small brown stone and carried it in a little pillbox in my pocket for years.

In a canyon we liked to hike, a spot beside the trail pulled at me every time I passed. When I finally stopped there to explore, I discovered a small Ancestral Puebloan ruin. There have been innumerable times like that, when I let my feelings guide my feet, and they have taken me to a stacked stone wall or a scatter of pottery sherds or a coyote skull.

Once you get used to it, it can be fun. You can watch your energy and emotions change as you move across the land, savoring the differences of place, much like you might savor the flavors of different dishes. And of course, it's not always pleasant; some areas are heavy with darkness, and even positive places might contain spots with negative vibes.

The strong sense of place in our area meant that many days contained small, bright experiences that flashed us into the moment, much like the "wake-up" gongs embedded in Buddhist chants: almost stepping on a spotted faun lying in the grass, spotting a rainbow that came to earth in a field right beside a highway, watching horses dart across a road to visit a mare and colt waiting beside a fence on the other side. Often those startles came from a sudden glimpse of the sky. Especially during the monsoon season, we might say, "Look at that!" pointing to a sunset or a massive thunderhead or a sky filled with cumulus clouds like a harbor crowded with white sails. Other times we'd glimpse red evening sunlight on the walls of a canyon or moonlight draped like white sheets on the mesas. As painters know, different times and places embody very different qualities of light.

Even some of the most down-to-earth people sensed the Ramah area's abiding presence; the force of the beauty and power of the land there is difficult to ignore. Some of it seems to flow from the Natives, whose ancestors go back thousands of years, and the Spaniards, Mexicans, and Mormons, whose lives and bones remain anchored in the soil. It is also embedded in the geology, natural history, and illuminating sunlight and brilliant night stars.

Many traditional Native American belief systems recognize the spiritual life of all things, animate and inanimate. There in the land of the Puebloans and Navajo it is easy to believe. In the words of the Irish poet and philosopher John O'Donohue, "The silence of the landscape conceals vast presence. Place is not simply location. A place is a profound individuality. . . . The shape of a landscape is an ancient and silent form of consciousness . . . The earth is full of soul." And therein, I believe, lies the essence of our beloved querencia.

20. The Old Zuni Mission

ZUNI WAS THE PUEBLO closest to our home, twenty-two miles west of Ramah on Highway 53. Zuni is the name of the tribe, the reservation, and their largest town. The town of Zuni has schools, shops, and modern houses, and in its center stands an old Spanish mission and a cluster of brown adobe homes, some of which have been inhabited for hundreds of years. There, in the ancient part of the town, the people's long history and tradition are anchored.

In Zuni a civilization steeped in history still very much lives. Clans and kivas and priest societies are active, and the people speak the Zuni language. Zuni people fast to honor the earth and their ancestors, dance for various religious and cultural purposes, and celebrate Shalako and other traditions unique to them. Seriously participating in the spiritual life of the community requires significant personal sacrifice and commitment.

Old tales woven into Zuni culture often relate to specific physical locations. They know, for example, exactly where their people emerged from the darkness inside the earth out to the light of day. Also, like the pueblo of Acoma and many other societies and religions, Zuni has a great flood story, and in theirs they can point to where it occurred. Theirs took place on Dowa Yalanne, also referred to as Corn Mountain, a large mesa just outside the pueblo. According to the tale, the Zuni were trapped there in a great storm and, as the water rose toward the top of the mesa, the desperate people sacrificed the daughter and son of a Zuni priest by throwing them into the raging water.

The gods were appeased, the flood receded, and the two children were honored by being turned to stone on the mesa rim. I told this story to our grandson Kenny and for quite a while thereafter, whenever he visited and we drove into Zuni, he would ask me to point out the two stone pillars at the top of Dowa Yalanne and tell their tale again.

When the Spanish took control of Zuni they used forced Indian labor to build a Catholic mission that was completed in 1629 and named Our Lady of Guadalupe. It still stands in the town square after almost four hundred years, an imposing structure that partially collapsed and was rebuilt. In front of the mission is a small, gated courtyard filled with old graves. Its windows and doors are framed with huge, wood beams, and a bell tower adorns its thick, brown plastered walls. Blood was spilled there when the conscripted Zuni people built it, and again when a Spanish priest was killed inside during the Pueblo Revolt of 1680.

One chilly, gray day in April we took a couple of visiting friends to see Zuni and its old mission, especially the murals painted and still in process on the walls inside. When we pulled up to the small wooden door on its side, we saw a few other folks, tourists from Florida and New York, waiting to enter. They told us they had phoned the church office a couple of blocks away and someone was coming over with a key to let us in. We waited beside our cars in the center of that ancient pueblo, smelling the fragrant piñon wood smoke from the fires in the old houses around the square and watching the dogs and children living their lives.

After a few minutes a young Zuni boy came running up to us and said, "They're dancing!" This was an unexpected and welcome surprise—a dance had begun in the small plaza near the church. We had never attended a Zuni dance, but that day we would. Although the Zuni dance fairly often, they don't have a set schedule because the religious leaders of the tribe usually don't announce dances until the morning of their occurrence.

We walked into the alley between the mission and the dance plaza and sure enough, in the courtyard at the alley's end, one of the kiva religious societies was performing a rain dance. Thirty or so men clad in deerskin moccasins, brightly colored outfits, and blue and red masks chanted, shaking rattles and moving in curving lines that wove sinuously around the small space.

The society of the dancers we watched had existed for hundreds, perhaps thousands, of years. The dancers had put on their costumes and performed on that day as a religious practice, to bring blessings to their village. Their kiva society (a kiva is a religious and social structure, usually circular and underground) was one of six that danced from season to season, for rain and other purposes.

We felt honored to witness this ancient religious rite and listen to the chanted song as we leaned against the brown adobe wall in the gray, chilly afternoon light. Someone whispered that, as non-Zuni, we should be watching from the roof of a building on the other side of the square, but we couldn't get there while the dance continued, so we stood where we were with three or four other tourists and looked on.

Eventually a woman from the Catholic Church office arrived and opened the mission. We entered, still able to hear the dancing and chanting as it continued outside. The inside of the mission was a single high room filled with old wooden pews and a loft at the back. Our eyes immediately closed in on the murals that covered the two long side walls of the church.

Depicted in life-size were dozens of the katsinas of the Zuni religion and priests, dancers, and others performing tribal religious functions. Traditional Zuni life is complex, and katsinas, divine and ancestral spirit beings, are prominent figures in their spiritual beliefs. They are powerful manifestations who bring good to their people, from rain to healing, abundant crops to protection.

On the left wall were paintings of warm month ceremonies, such as rain dances and initiation rites, along with an altar of a medicine priest, all beneath a blue sky topped by a rainbow and a plumed serpent. Birds, plants, and a bright sun graced a procession of katsinas.

The murals on the right wall depicted winter, including an image of the Shalako, the namesake katsina at the center of their most iconic ceremony of the year. Alongside the Shalako were Mudheads, Longhorns, a Shalako priest, and other katsinas of the cold months. Above them stretched a gray sky and at their feet lay snow, all glittering with frost.

Alex Seowtewa, a Zuni man, began painting the scenes in 1970 when he convinced a Catholic priest that despite his lack of artistic training, he could create beautiful images on the mission walls. He wanted to depict the traditional Zuni religion in this Catholic space and preserve images of Zuni culture that might otherwise disappear. Traditional Zuni priest functions can be lost forever if a priest dies before he has a chance to teach his chants and songs to another.

Alex could often be found with two of his sons, Ken and Gerald, painting in the mission, high on scaffolding against a wall or up in the loft where they worked on a large panel that depicted the church as it was many years ago. At the top of the panel reigned a Zuni Christ figure, pouring corn pollen blessings upon the church and town below.

Although they weren't there on that day of our visit, Alex and his sons would pause mid-painting to explain their work to interested visitors. We remembered when, on previous visits to the mission, they had patiently talked about their religious beliefs, the significance of each depicted figure, and the tribe's cruel domination by the Spanish. The Seowtewas were committed men, engaged in a lifelong, creative passion.

In addition to recording aspects of their culture, their work was a purging of the energy of Spanish paintings that had once been there. In the mid-1800s the Catholic priests had ordered that the mission walls display paintings of disciplinarian katsinas, as warnings to members of the tribe of punishments that would be meted out if they failed to attend services.

Sadly, though, the Seowtewas' paintings are in danger. The plaster upon which they rest is separating from the walls, and despite several proposals over the years, no organization has come forth with the necessary funds and a viable solution.

We visitors stood in the back and listened to the faint droning of the church representative at the front as it intertwined with the muffled chants and rattles of the dancers outside. I thought about the irony of glimpsing this ancient Indigenous culture and considering it something unusual, when, in fact, my presence was the exotic in this space deeply indigenous to the local people.

The rain dancers continued to move to rhythms rooted in time and earth, and we went back outside to where a light rain had indeed begun to fall. Finally, the dancers walked to a nearby house to eat and rest, weaving through a cluster of automobiles in which Zuni people sat and watched the dancers from behind rain-streaked windows.

As I reflect on that time when we stood in the Zuni rain amid all the tumult of the world, I am struck by the contrasts: between us observers and the Zuni, and between the ancient and modern worlds inhabited by the Zuni themselves. A question I heard somewhere long ago comes to mind—How do we belong together?—and I think the way we answer is something upon which the future of all of us depends.

21. Shalako

SHALAKO, ONE OF ZUNI'S most significant ceremonial events, begins just before the winter solstice in early December, on a date set by the Zuni bow priests. It marks the return of the katsinas, including the namesake Shalako katsinas, from the hills to the village where they will spend the winter.

The culminating night of the week-long celebration falls on a Saturday, and in years past the ceremony has been open to visitors, but outsiders became so intrusive that these days Shalako is usually a closed event. We were told that the final straw was a foreign tourist who jumped in front of a Shalako figure during the ceremony to take flash pictures.

The first time we attended Shalako we and our friend Cheryl were invited to dinner by a Zuni family, which allowed us entrance. Like many replanted residents, Cheryl ended up in the Ramah area through a process of self-re-creation. She had owned two hair salons in Virginia, sold them, and then a series of adventures landed her in our vicinity where she built a geodesic dome house near Ramah Lake.

When we first moved to the area we went on explorations with her and learned a great deal about the people and the lay of the land. Cheryl knew almost everybody and every place and led us on excursions where we couldn't believe our trusty Ford Explorer could go. A vivacious lady with short blonde hair and a bright grin, she had a happy Lab named Dusty who made a great companion for our Lab/Basset, Walter. She would call and say, "Are you ready for an adventure?" and off we'd traipse to a remote waterfall, a special spot high in the Zuni mountains, or canyons and mountaintops and hills all over.

On the big night of Shalako the three of us headed into Zuni through lightly falling snow to try to find our dinner host's home. He'd given Cheryl directions, but they weren't very clear. We wandered around here and there, scanning for cars Cheryl knew would be parked outside. The town had an eerie feeling as we drove slowly up and down the streets. It was cold and the wind swept the light snow in swirls around the houses. A number of the homes had fires in front or behind them, and we could sometimes see backlit figures standing or sitting near the flames. We finally found our host's house and knocked on the door, but no one answered.

Even though it was 6:00 p.m., the time for our arrival, we decided to go back to the main drag and grab a bite from Taco Bell. Maybe our host and his family had changed their plans and there wouldn't be dinner at their house after all. The Taco Bell in Zuni was inside a grocery store/gas station, with a few booths tucked in a back corner. We sat quietly munching our tacos, watching people come into the bright store from the dark, snowy evening. Most were Zuni but a few Anglos wandered in and out, looking a little confused and excited.

When we finished we decided to drive by the elementary school. Cheryl had heard that something was to take place there, but we were really just wandering to kill time. We passed some streets with blockades manned by Zuni police, which we later learned were the areas where the Shalakos would come into town from across the river, and only Zuni were allowed. We approached the school and found ourselves in a long, crawling line of cars, then parked on a side street and walked across snowy fields to a house with visible activity.

A Shalako, a figure nine or ten feet tall with a large, painted wooden head and a long, narrow beak, stood in front of the house. It vaguely resembled an enormous bird with a fanned crest of feathers and a bushy ruff around its neck. Its long, cone-shaped body was white and black with colored designs on it, and it was draped with feathers.

A small crowd of Zuni people surrounded the Shalako, in the midst of which a group of men chanted and sang in the Zuni language. As they chanted the Shalako swayed and loudly clacked his beak. Eventually, the Shalako bent down and entered the home, followed by the people. We saw him through the windows, standing as tall as the ceiling, swaying and clacking. We returned to the car and drove back to our dinner house, hoping our host had returned.

This time when we knocked our host, Tony, opened the door, greeted us warmly, and invited us in. Dinner had already begun, so after introductions everyone scrunched close together to give us room around the table. The people were gracious and on the night of Shalako folks are especially open and sharing. Even though we knew almost no one, we felt totally welcome.

Dinner was attended by the three of us, plus eight or nine family members. Food was served family style, with big bowls of roast beef, ham, potatoes, green beans, carrots, onions, Jell-O salad, and lots of bread. They gave us plates and encouraged us to reach out and take what we wanted, and the food was delicious, capped by generous portions of banana and chocolate cream pies. The conversation was animated and noisy with two television sets on in the background, one in the living room and one in the dining room.

We asked a few questions, including how the Zuni related to the Catholic Church. We were aware that in many of the pueblos religion might include both traditional beliefs and the Catholicism imposed on them by the Spaniards in the 1600s. A pueblo may, for instance, celebrate a saint's day when they honor their patron saint with a Catholic Mass, but the rites may be performed in their native tongue and the celebration continued with traditional dancing, ceremonies, and feasting, as at the Laguna Pueblo. We were told that Zuni is less Catholic than many of the other pueblos, in part because they sharply remember the abuse they suffered at the hands of the Spanish invaders.

Tony had told Cheryl earlier that he would not say much about the meaning of what we would see at Shalako, and he was true to his word. When I mentioned that we had noticed in his yard, like those of many houses in Zuni, a fire, he said, "I'm just barbequing." Another person laughed and said, "Actually, the fires are to honor our ancestors."

After dinner, as we sat in the living room, we began to hear drumming and chanting coming from down the block. Lucia asked about it and our host said that a Shalako house was nearby. Each year the Zuni build several Shalako houses, new houses to be blessed by the Shalako. That year they had built seven, and the central events throughout the night took place in them. There Shalako, Mudheads, and Longhorns danced, food was served, and people gathered until dawn.

By then it was about ten in the evening, and we decided to leave. We thought we'd go home, but Tony recommended that we visit the Shalako house. When we told him we were reluctant to intrude, he said, "No, you should go, you will be welcome there. And you should eat some food; if you don't, it will be like a rejection of their hospitality." We decided to follow his recommendation and drove to a Shalako house, parked, and wandered toward the front door. As we approached a female voice from an unseen face in the dark offered friendly advice: "Don't go in the front door; go around to the back." We walked around to the back door and entered.

We found ourselves in a house with two long rooms, each with rows of folding chairs. The rooms flanked either side of a narrow space that ran between them, which was where the ceremonies would occur. The room we entered also had a kitchen area and a large table where Zuni women kept bowls and platters filled with mutton stew, bread, and a variety of other dishes. Around the table some twenty chairs sat an ever-changing group of people who would eat, then make way for others. Folks encouraged us to sit down, but we didn't want to take up seats needed by hungry people, so we stood, looked around, and snacked for a while on cookies and Coke.

Deer heads hung with turquoise jewelry decorated the ceremonial space between our room and the one on the other side, and colorful pieces of cloth hung from the ceiling. At one end of the space stood an altar and chairs for the drummers and chanters. Because the tall Shalako would dance in the ceremonial space, a channel in the floor had been dug lower to accommodate it. After the celebration folks would fill it back in before the house was inhabited.

We stood at the back of the room and waited, leaning against the wall. Eventually we sat, and nothing much happened for the next three hours. People came and went, ate and talked, or napped in the chairs around us. In all that time we saw only five or six other Anglos: a schoolteacher Cheryl knew from Zuni; an older Californian couple who were, like us, guests of a Zuni family; and two or three others who seemed at home as they sat at the table, ate mutton stew, and chatted.

Sitting tired and sleepy in the chairs and watching life go gently on was a rich part of the experience. As the night continued we began to appreciate the power of all-night religious events such as this. Exhaustion and the long waiting time tended to put us in an altered and receptive state for the ceremonies to come. Throughout the evening we could see people outside, wandering around in the snowy dark and bitter cold, squinting into the windows and blowing on their hands.

At about 12:45 a.m. the drummers came in, dressed in their Native garb and ready for action. They situated themselves in their chairs and then, like the rest of us, settled down to wait. After fifteen minutes or so they took down rattles that hung above them on the wall, and the young man next to us, an Anglo schoolteacher at the Zuni school, told us that this was a good sign. "It won't be long now," he said.

Finally, the Shalako priest entered and the drummers began. In bright garb and painted face, the priest danced up and down in the channel, facing us and then the people in the chairs across from us in the other room. He danced sideways, usually with his eyes closed and his staff moving to the rhythmic drum and chant. Next, a Shalako entered. Here came a figure like the one we saw at the first Shalako house, nine or ten feet tall with a brightly painted head and a long, narrow, clacking wooden beak, hung with turquoise jewelry and dancing to the drumbeat.

Together the priest and the Shalako danced back and forth, facing us and then the people on the other side. On and on the dance went, and we understood that they would dance throughout the village all night. Now that the dancing had begun, the Shalako, Mudheads, Longhorns, and priests would go from house to house and continue dancing until dawn. Everyone in our house and the people looking through the windows watched quietly as the priest and the Shalako danced.

When it got to be about 3:00 a.m., that was it for us: We were exhausted and decided to go home. We knew that at some point the Longhorns and Mudheads and others would appear, but we were out of steam. We worked our way through the crowded room and out the door, going from the overheated brightness we had inhabited for so long into the sharp cold outside.

As we crunched over the snow to our car and drove home in the early morning dark, we imagined how tired the men who animated the Shalako would be after dancing all night, only to begin the next day by racing in a field near the center of the pueblo, as they do every year.

The world of the Zuni, and generally of traditional Indigenous people everywhere, is very different from mine. I wouldn't trade my way of life for theirs, but I would welcome a culture so infused with spiritual connection to nature, ancestors, and community. Despite their many difficulties, an enduring bond runs like a deep river through the Zuni Pueblo, and they are some of the most good-hearted people we've met anywhere. As visitors to Shalako and other Native ceremonies, we always felt grateful and tried to honor the welcome extended to us with humility and respect.

22. Santo Niño

SANTO NIÑO RESIDES IN Zuni Pueblo in the small adobe house of the family that has sheltered her continuously for hundreds of years. She is an ancient and revered santo in a humble setting: a narrow, rectangular room with old couches and chairs lined up along the sides.

Christian and Zuni religious pictures and symbols adorn the walls, and a pedestal sits at the end of the room. On the pedestal is a clear plastic enclosure that contains Santo Niño, a wooden carving of the Christ child. About eighteen inches tall, she is painted with bright enamel, garbed in fancy dresses and children's shoes, and ornamented with turquoise and silver jewelry. She has a pouch at her side for visitors' gifts.

There is a disconnect here. The Christ child and the Spanish term "Santo Niño" are both masculine, but the Zuni clothe and address the carving as female. Although she originated as a representation of baby Jesus and remains so to Catholics, to the Zuni she is the daughter of the Sun Father.

Her history goes back hundreds of years and is connected to the story of a Muslim Moroccan named Esteban de Dorantes, the first person to make contact between Spain and the Zuni people. In fact, he was the first non-Indian to set foot anywhere in the American Southwest. As pueblo historian and member of Jemez Pueblo Joe Sando said, "The first white man our people saw was a black man."

Esteban was born around 1503, probably in the Moroccan city of Azemmour. In his late teens he was acquired as a slave by Portuguese merchants, sold to a Spanish nobleman, and eventually he and his owner became part of a Spanish expedition to seek gold and other valuables in Florida. At that point he had probably been converted to Catholicism, as Spain only allowed Catholics to travel to the New World.

The trials and adventures of Esteban are epic. The expedition of which he was a part was decimated by hurricanes, starvation, illness, and battles with Natives. Then the remnants of the expedition became scattered, and Esteban and a few others were enslaved for several years by Coahuiltecan Indians in the area of what is now southern Texas.

He and three Spaniards eventually escaped and after some time the four of them, including the explorer Cabeza de Vaca, became celebrated traveling medicine men among the Native people. They were called "the children of the sun" and given food, lavish gifts, and shelter, and were so revered that sometimes large groups of Natives would follow them for miles as they traveled from village to village.

In 1536 they began to hear rumors of Spanish slavers in the area and the four "healers" searched out the group of Spaniards, who led them back to their leadership in Mexico City. A couple of years later the Spanish sent out an exploratory expedition to what is now New Mexico in search of the treasures of the fabled Seven Cities of Cibola, and because of his Native language skills and familiarity with the region and its tribes, Esteban was sent along as translator and guide.

Fray Marcos, a Franciscan priest, was designated nominal leader of the expedition. He directed Esteban to take a few Native men ahead a couple of days to explore the route and arrange for food and accommodations for the priest and others who followed. Eventually Esteban arrived at the place his Indian followers said was one of the Seven Cities of Cibola, the Zuni village of Hawikuh.

When he arrived at Hawikuh, Esteban sent a message into the village that he was a representative of a great white king to whom they were now subject and that they must worship the king's god and give him tribute. And this is the last of what reliable history reveals about Esteban.

Some historians claim that the Zuni killed Esteban, and others speculate that he slipped quietly away to avoid continued enslavement. Whatever happened, the mystery of his end remains an engaging intrigue for historians of the Southwest.

Esteban's story is truly remarkable. He was enslaved by Arabs and then became a slave of the Portuguese, then the Spanish, then Native Americans, and finally the Spanish again. A natural polyglot, he spoke Arabic, Spanish, and several Indigenous languages, and provided a vital communication bridge between the Spanish and the Indian tribes. He was the first person from the Old World to cross the North American continent and the first from outside the continent to explore the Americana Southwest.

Despite the fact that he altered the trajectory and culture of the New World, though, recorded history only faintly traces his story. As Dennis Herrick points out in his excellent and engaging book *Esteban*, his status as a slave, and perhaps the color of his skin, consequently minimized the significance of his historical role.

After Esteban disappeared, Fray Marcos, who never got anywhere near Hawikuh, returned to Mexico City and wrote a report stating that the village held great riches. Based on the friar's statements, and with his guidance, Coronado set off on his famous entrada north into what is now the United States.

When Coronado and his soldiers reached the Zuni area in 1540, they promptly attacked and conquered Hawikuh, giving the village the dubious distinction of being the first Native pueblo conquered by Spain. Although they found no treasure, the Spanish remained occupiers and harsh rulers for 140 years.

In 1628 the Spanish constructed La Purísima Concepción Mission in Hawikuh, and Santo Niño entered the scene a year later when Franciscan friars placed the carving, brought from Spain, in the mission.

Four years after the mission's construction the residents of Hawikuh rebelled against the Spanish, burned the church, and killed the priest. The mission was rebuilt and then burned again, this time by Apache raiders. It was rebuilt and burned for the third and last time by the Zuni during the Great Pueblo Revolt of 1680, in which most of the pueblos joined together and threw the Spanish completely out of the area. After that the Zuni permanently depopulated the village of Hawikuh.

Santo Niño survived the first two burnings of the Hawikuh mission and in 1670, ten years before the last burning, the carving was moved to the town of Zuni and ensconced in the Nuestra Señora de Guadalupe Mission. That structure, like the Hawikuh mission, was burned in the 1680 revolt, but the carving continued its charmed existence. Before the Zuni people burned the mission they removed and saved Santo Niño, along with the priest's vestments and other items. Different versions of the history of Santo Niño arose over the next couple of centuries, but at some point after 1680 she was moved to the small, flat-roofed house where she resides today.

Catholic reverence for her as a Christ-child icon goes back a long way. People traveled to see her over the decades by horseback, wagon, car, and on foot, seeking blessings and expressing gratitude for healings and other boons. They still come, sometimes on walking pilgrimages of many miles. People even travel from other countries to visit the sacred relic in its humble dwelling, attracted by her reputed power to heal. One day, when we were visiting Santo Niño, two men arrived on a pilgrimage from Arizona. As we sat on the couches, they knelt and prayed for a while and placed an offering in her pouch before they left.

To Zuni she is sacred as the daughter of the Sun Father. Although the practice has faded, in the past she was honored each year at the harvest celebration in the main plaza, where she was carried in procession and attended by members of the tribal council. Young women decked out in traditional finery festooned with turkey plumes, blue macaw feathers, and ribbons danced to chanting and drums. The festivities culminated in a huge giveaway by the tribal governor, who tossed squash, pumpkins, cloth, bread, and other items to the crowd.

There are numerous Zuni stories of Santo Niño's blessings and activities. She is credited with the safe return of Zuni soldiers, the healing of wounds and diseases, and the granting of other prayers. Zuni mothers place her dresses and shoes on their children as protection against injury and illness, and it is said that she walks around at night performing miracles, which is why her shoes wear out and must be regularly replaced. Folks say she loves coffee, so sometimes coffee stains appear on her dress, and occasionally you can spot ice cream stains as well.

All that remains today of Hawikuh, one of the most ancient and historic settlements in America and Santo Niño's first home, are scattered piles of stone and a few wall outlines. We visited there many years ago, driving down a series of dirt roads and only knowing we had arrived because of a small handmade sign. You can go there today, but only with a Zuni guide, which helps protect the integrity of the site.

I find it remarkable and good that both Hawikuh and Santo Niño, such significant relics of the inhabitants of this land, are not more widely known and celebrated. Their quiet repose allows their mystery and spirit to continue and helps the resonance of this beloved place remain strong, free from the trammels of the modern world.

23. Horny and Spadefoot

AMONG THE INHABITANTS OF this area are two remarkable cold-blooded creatures. The first has fascinated me since I was a boy catching them on the Kansas prairie, and they still do when we find them here in New Mexico. We call them horny toads or horned toads, but they aren't toads at all; they are horned lizards. And even though sharp spikes cover their flat, stumpy bodies, making them look like fierce, tiny dinosaurs, they are actually quite docile and easily caught.

Horned lizards rely on the camouflage of their coloration to protect themselves, varying from shades of yellow, red, and brown to almost black. They cannot run fast, but when they run in short bursts and stop suddenly, their camouflage makes them seem to disappear. If that doesn't work, they have other defenses; they inflate like spiky pufferfish to make themselves difficult for predators to swallow or they flop on their back and play dead.

The most unusual thing about them, though, is their ability to eject a stream of blood for six or seven feet from their eyes. This is an especially good defense against dogs and coyotes, as horned lizard blood contains a substance canines abhor. They do it by reducing the blood pressure in their heads and increasing it in their eyes until tiny blood vessels in the corner of their eyes burst. In all the years I have watched these lizards I have never seen them do this.

When I was young I briefly kept one as a pet. At one point I was in the hospital with a bad case of poison ivy, and my sister brought me my horned lizard to keep me company. One morning, when he was napping on my breakfast tray, a woman came in and picked it up. As she walked away she glanced down and saw the lizard beside the empty plate, staring up at her in his characteristic cocked-head position. She screamed, dropped the tray, and ran straight out of the room. I jumped up and got him back in his box, and later my parents took him outside and set him free.

I wasn't aware of any repercussions from the episode, but I imagine sometimes what would have happened if he had shot her with a stream of blood. She probably would have required extensive therapy, and I would still be barred from the hospital premises.

When they aren't squirting blood, horned lizards enjoy munching on their primary food, harvester ants. Dying harvester ants emit a smell that brings other ants on the attack, and the lizards take advantage of this. They sit beside ant trails, munch a few, then gobble up others as they rally to the scent.

Sadly they are becoming rarer, in part because harvester ant populations are being reduced by invasive ant species. Also, their habitat is shrinking, and too many people keep them as pets. Horned lizards don't make good pets because of their specialized diet, which means they usually starve in captivity.

The New Mexico state amphibian, the spadefoot toad, is every bit as interesting as the horned lizard. During our first New Mexico summer, after the rainy season had begun, a sound like the opening and closing of a bunch of creaky doors enveloped us in the evenings. I wandered around unsuccessfully in the grass with a flashlight trying to locate the source of the noise that lasted for a few more nights and then disappeared.

Later, folks told us that we had just experienced our first encounter with what the locals call "singing toads." All male toads and frogs vocalize during their mating season to attract females, so their croaking is normal to hear around lakes and wetlands. We just didn't expect to hear them in our desert backyard.

For many creatures, plants and animals alike, living in arid places is somewhat like being a bush pilot in Alaska. Long periods pass when almost nothing happens, interspersed with short bursts of frantic activity. The bursts of desert life occur during the short rainy season, which explains why desert flowers explode into bloom all at once.

Spadefoots need water in which to lay their eggs so their eggs can hatch and become tadpoles. Then the tadpoles must grow and metamorphize from swimming creatures with gills into toads with lungs. That's some trick to pull off when the rainy season here only lasts for a few weeks and the water that pools may only last a matter of days.

Part of the success of spadefoot toads is indicated by their name, which comes from the spade-shaped protrusions on their hind legs that they use to dig themselves backward into the earth. In a normal dry season they go down six or seven feet and hibernate for ten months or so, but in times of extended drought they can remain there for several years. When they sense thunder or rain they quickly emerge from the earth, and the males immediately begin singing for mates. Their voices are loud and carry for up to two miles, so females far away in their burrows can hear them.

After breeding the females lay their eggs, and the eggs hatch in as little as twenty-four hours. Then the tadpoles eat and grow, doubling their weight every two days, and they go through the vital metamorphosis that will give them lungs in about two weeks. This is among the fastest metamorphoses of any amphibian. If they don't complete their lung development before the ponds dry out, then, of course, the tadpoles die.

I read somewhere that because spadefoots come up to breed

when they feel the vibrations of thunder, the rumble of passing trucks causes some of them in the vicinity of highways to emerge at the wrong time, and as a result, they die. That's quite a macabre image: desiccated bodies of hoodwinked toads scattered all along the New Mexico highway corridors. We've never seen it, and we hope we never do.

24. Growers

WITH ITS LOW RAINFALL and high altitude, the Ramah area seems an unlikely location for the production of organic food. The "you can count on it," frost-free growing season only lasts about three months. Wide swings of temperature between day and night frequently cause new plants and blossoms to freeze, and it takes a lot of acreage per cow to raise beef. Bees have to be regularly fed, and without constant vigilance surges of insects can quickly decimate gardens.

Commitment, intelligence, and flexibility, however, can apparently overcome these obstacles, because the place is dense with organic gardeners and home to two commercial producers of organic, grass-fed beef.

Organic growers in the Ramah area tend to be firmly rooted in the natural environment and attuned to the weather and the turnings of the earth—which they must be. When the rains don't come they have to pump water from a well or haul it in on a truck, and they can't ignore insects because they don't bathe their crops in prophylactic toxins. Rather than following rote processes, they must constantly work within the rapidly shifting systems of nature.

Denis and Jackie are great examples of this. Their place, Hobbit Gardens, sits on five acres with plantings in fields and greenhouses. They regularly add new varieties of salad greens to their offerings at the Ramah Farmers Market and the co-op in Gallup. Fresh eggs from chickens and ducks are usually available, and they raise turkeys and rabbits and have a horse for farm work.

Their operation is guided by an intimate knowledge of the chemistry of their land and how it varies from place to place. Soil is enriched and balanced with natural ingredients, with a goal of adding nothing except substances that originally come from their land. They network around the state and elsewhere on issues related to organic food production and are eager to explain what they do and why. During the years we lived outside of Ramah they were the primary managers of both the Ramah Farmers Market and the local organic growers newsletter called *The Farmer's Beet*.

When we wanted produce from Hobbit Gardens we'd give them a call and put some money in our mailbox that Jackie and Denis would replace with a dozen eggs, spinach, lettuce, and mixed greens. Three or four people sold fresh eggs at the farmers market or Kate's feed store in El Morroville, but we liked Denis and Jackie's eggs the best; they had a deep, rich taste much different from regular store-bought eggs that arrive several weeks old. We really miss those Ramah eggs.

Owl, another local organic produce grower, calls his place Whoo-Ville Farm, and it contains a series of greenhouses, gardens, and walkways that meander through beds of flowers. He is an innovator and has developed a process for generating a liquid inoculate, a mix of microorganisms for creating and maintaining healthy, living soil. He has several projects, including a website, Internet courses, and a book, all to spread the word about his system of microbiome compost gardening and regenerative agriculture. He is also a skilled potter, one of several in the area.

Owl volunteers with a not-for-profit called Work in Beauty, which owns and manages a ten-acre agricultural learning and experimental center. They hold events and workshops almost every weekend from the end of March through October, and they often have thirty or more attendees. Subjects include holistic orchard management, rainwater harvesting, erosion control, permaculture, and soil mycology.

Management of rainwater is always a major focus because even with accessible well water, rainwater is best for gardens for a variety of reasons. On most plots of land rainwater retention can be significantly improved by the alteration of the topography with berms, catchments, and swales that channel and catch water and allow it to percolate into the soil.

Growers in this difficult climate tend to look for opportunities in the challenges they face. On the Work in Beauty land, for example, an arroyo became enlarged because of occasional heavy rainfall events, until it threatened to wash away the road. This was a bad thing that needed correcting, but it also presented an opportunity to demonstrate effective techniques for rainwater management. Owl and his compadres constructed swales along the arroyo to spread rainwater out onto the land, slowing its flow so it had time to soak into the soil, thus stabilizing the condition of the road.

The outdoor Ramah Farmers Market takes place each Saturday during the growing season, and we always had fun going because so many of our friends attended as vendors or customers. Will and Pam sold a product from the chile they grow called Willie's Chiles, a spicy blend of sliced peppers in thick, sweet syrup. Kristi sold bouquets of mixed flowers, Jack sold home-raised gladiolas, and Kate usually sold out of her vegetables, especially her delicious red and white radishes. In addition to vegetables and salad makings, the market's offerings include pottery, baked goods, homemade soap, jewelry, carvings, and art. You could also find folk singer performances, campfire coffee, and games for the kids.

When the market moved its location from the edge of town to its current spot in front of the Ramah Museum, Ramah folks welcomed it with open arms. Even though the market brought into town a bevy of people with a wide variety of beliefs and lifestyles, gardening helped bridge the differences. The Ramah Mormon community has a long tradition of growing, canning, and sharing food, which fits nicely with the hippie, back-to-the-land vibe that began flowing into the area in the 1960s.

Regular social events help organic gardeners support each other and share advice and experiences. Such events include workshops on beekeeping and fruit tree cultivation, seed exchanges, and harvest potlucks. The Ancient Way Fall Festival, described in the chapter "Folk Music," is the grower's signature happening, with produce sales and contests for the best homesteading display, most beautiful chicken, and weirdest vegetable shape. For many of these folks gardening isn't just a hobby; it's the way they live.

Kate of delicious radish fame is an example of someone for whom organic gardening has become a central part of her identity. When she talks about her garden she becomes poetic. She says that one of the blessings of the harsh environment is that it holds gardeners in attention to and harmony with nature.

Her garden includes fruit trees, and she keeps bees and raises angora rabbits. Yet her bees don't give her much honey because flowers for nectar only bloom for a short time each year. In fact, the bees barely make enough honey to sustain themselves, and sometimes she has to feed them sugar water. Additionally, Kate's fruit trees seldom bear fruit. Locals say that fruit trees in Ramah only bear fruit once every seven years because late-season freezes usually kill the blossoms.

I asked her once why she raises bees and fruit trees if they seldom give her honey and fruit. She laughed and said that her garden isn't just for her personal benefit. Her bees are important pollinators as wild bee populations diminish, and her fruit trees amend the soil by increasing its fungal content.

Kate also creates with felt and spins wool from the hair of her angora rabbits. She loves to spin; it is a hypnotic process that unwinds and quiets her. Her sister in Vermont has sheep, so together they send their wool to a commercial facility that spins the angora and sheep wool together into yarn. She doesn't spin the combined wool herself, she said, because there is just too much of it.

She added that farmers markets in the Southwest are, on average, more financially successful than those in the Midwest, partly because the harsh climate in the Southwest makes growing vegetables in backyard gardens so challenging. I thought about the truth of her statement. When I lived in Iowa, where growing requires little effort, backyard vegetable gardens were everywhere. Someone there once told me that I shouldn't leave my car unlocked in late summer because the back seat would quickly fill up with zucchinis.

Even within a generally peaceful, earth-connected community, conflict will occasionally rise. One such instance involved Charlie, an organic, grass-fed beef producer. One year, rather than loading his cattle on a truck and carting them to a different pasture via a long round-about road, he thought it would be better to herd them directly. He asked an adjacent homeowners association if he could stage a cattle drive across their commons and the association board agreed, seeing it as a colorful event and a good-neighbor thing to do. Some landowners, however, were strongly opposed, and things got so hot between the two groups that the sheriff was called out during the drive to prevent physical confrontations.

Another time, a landowner in Ramah sold a parcel for the construction of a dollar store. Many people approved of the idea because the store carried a variety of goods that previously required a trip to Gallup, but a few folks got angry because the store also carried unhealthy food such as candy, soda pop, and TV dinners. Eventually, the hard feelings faded and everybody settled their differences.

Many of us have an image of the American farmer as a man in

overalls and a straw hat, living with his family on the land they farm. He drives an old pickup and can fix almost anything with baling wire. He sees himself as the steward of his land and uses natural systems like crop rotation, letting fields lie fallow, and planting legumes to replenish the nitrogen in his soil. His profit margin, if he has one, is slim. He is buffeted by floods, droughts, and market prices, and we depend on him to grow our vegetables and raise our meat.

I knew such farmers when I was a boy in Kansas, but most of our food these days comes from large corporate farming operations whose only goal is profit. They apply pesticides on all their crops before insects or weeds can infest, and they blanket their fields with chemical fertilizer. As a result, bees are dying en masse, food is contaminated with chemicals, and the soil is losing its residual organic matter.

In some places, however, those early farming ways still thrive. Growers like those in Ramah don't just grow crops; they grow healthy food, and their soil is full of life.

25. Genízaros

THIRTY-FIVE MILES NORTH OF Santa Fe, New Mexico, Hispanic settlers established the small village of Abiquiú during the 1730s, on top of the ruins of a Tewa Pueblo dating back to the thirteenth century. Today Abiquiú is best known as the former home of the artist Georgia O'Keeffe. We traveled there one weekend to explore, and on our first evening, as we walked up the steps onto the wooden porch of a restaurant, we encountered a dignified, white-haired man sitting in a wooden chair with a few copies of a book in his lap.

His name was Napoleon Garcia, and he told us his book, *The Genízaro and the Artist*, chronicled his many years working for O'Keeffe as a jack-of-all-trades. We purchased a copy and he invited us to his home the next day, where he promised to spin tales of his life. This sounded interesting, so we thanked him and accepted his offer.

The next morning we drove to his house in Abiquiú, where it sat amid a cluster of small homes surrounding the dusty plaza adjacent to an old adobe Catholic church. Mr. Garcia greeted us at the door and offered us seats on the porch, where a couple from New York already sat with glasses of iced tea. He eased himself into his chair and began recounting tales of his life and his relationship with the famous artist. He was a gracious and natural storyteller, and although his O'Keeffe tales interested us, we were particularly arrested by his statement that he was a Genízaro, something of which we had never heard.

Today's Genízaros are descendants of Native people who were enslaved long ago. They were mostly Plains Indians, captured in intertribal warfare by other Plains tribes and sold to Spaniards to work in their homes and fields. An important source of labor, they could be purchased at annual trade fairs held in the New Mexico towns of Pecos, Taos, and Abiquiú. In the 1740s Fray Pedro Serrano referred to them as "the richest treasure for the governor." Although purchased primarily by the Spanish, some were also sold to other Native groups.

Because the slavery of Indians was illegal under Spanish law, Genízaros were classified as indentured servants who would supposedly be freed when they became Christianized and worked long enough to pay back the cost of their purchase. For all practical purposes, though, they weren't indentured servants; they were slaves.

Indentured servitude has existed worldwide for thousands of years; it was a means by which many Europeans managed to move to the British North American colonies. Someone in the colonies usually paid for their fare in exchange for their labor for a specified amount of time. The Genízaros, though, did not sign up voluntarily and were sometimes never released during their lifetimes. Both slavery and indentured servitude were abolished in the United States shortly after the end of the Civil War, by ratification of the Thirteenth Amendment to the US Constitution in 1865.

Mr. Garcia also said that his home sat on a Spanish land grant created in 1754. The grant consisted of approximately 1,600 acres and was given to a community of thirty-four Genízaro families. The Spanish intended to create a buffer from nomadic Indians, especially Ute and Comanche, who had raided Abiquiú almost to the point of its abandonment.

Land grants in New Mexico go back as far as 1598 and were made by both the Spanish and the Mexican governments during their respective periods of control. Two kinds of land grants exist: private grants to individuals and grants to communities. Community grants, such as the one where Mr. Garcia lived, allowed small parcels for individual ownership, with the majority of the land held for common uses, such as farming and grazing.

The grants are still legally valid in the United States today because of the Treaty of Guadalupe-Hidalgo, which was signed at the conclusion of the Mexican American War in 1848. This treaty transferred 55 percent of the country of Mexico to the United States and also required that the United States recognize land grants made by the Spanish and Mexican governments. Currently, New Mexico contains twenty-two land grants, covering some two hundred thousand acres.

The relationship between the Abiquiú Genízaros and the Spanish did not run smoothly. In 1756, two years after the grant was established, some community members were accused of witchcraft and sorcery and placed on trial by the Spanish. The trials went on for ten years and resulted in the jailing and flogging of suspects and the destruction of icons and other items that the Spanish considered pagan idols.

Basically, the trials were part of the attempts by the Spanish to suppress Indigenous religious and cultural practices, including traditional methods of healing, in order to bring Native people more firmly in conformity with the Catholic faith. Although the Genízaros' traditional practices were reduced, they were not extinguished but driven underground.

Today Genízaros are found throughout northern New Mexico, particularly in Española, Taos, Santa Fe, Las Vegas, and the Albuquerque South Valley. Many are dispersed into the general population, but some, such as those at Abiquiú, have maintained their common history and culture. Although they may describe themselves as Hispanic, they also celebrate their unique Genízaro identities.

On the annual feast day of Santo Tomás in Abiquiú each November, for instance, children dance in Native garb to the beat of a hand drum and sing songs that include words no one can translate. The community also performs a small play that reenacts the process of being taken and sold as a slave. A prisoner is selected from the crowd, and someone calls out, "¿Quién lo conoce?" (Who knows this person?). Then someone else steps forward and ritually presents the purchase price.

In 2007 the New Mexico Legislature formally recognized Genízaros as Indigenous people and acknowledged the important role they and their descendants "have had in the social, economic, political, and cultural milieu of New Mexico and the United States." As that legislative action implies, Genízaros constitute, in many ways, a distinct Indigenous community, separate from other tribes in the country.

26. Los Hermanos Penitentes

ONE DAY IN LAS Vegas, New Mexico, a small city about an hour east of Santa Fe, we wandered into a shop on the town square that sold antiques and other miscellaneous items. Half hidden among other objects on a counter was an old, dusty mosaic made of Ancestral Puebloan pottery sherds glued to a wooden board. It roughly depicted the hill where Jesus was crucified, and the store owner referred to it as a Penitente work.

We bought it, and that was our first introduction to the religious group called Los Hermanos Penitentes. The group's impressive full name is Los Hermanos de la Fraternidad Piadosa de Nuestro Padre Jesús Nazareno. Like the Genízaros, the existence of the Penitentes in the Southwest is directly due to the long period of Spanish domination and the Catholicism they firmly rooted there.

The flourishing of the Penitentes, however, primarily resulted from the remarkably short period of Mexican rule in the area after the Spanish left. Our friend and neighbor in Timberlake David Weber, a premier expert on the Spanish empire in this hemisphere, stated in his book *The Mexican Frontier, 1821–1846*:

The flag of independent Mexico had flown over the Far North

only briefly. It rose in 1821 when Mexico won independence from Spain and began its fall a decade and a half later in Texas when that province successfully revolted in 1836. During the war with the United States in 1846–48, Mexican flags were lowered for the last time over California and New Mexico. A few years later, in 1854, when the United States Senate ratified the Gadsden purchase of a great strip of land below the Gila River, Mexico's flag ceased to fly in what we know today as Arizona.

Despite its brevity, Mexican control of the Southwest had lasting consequences, one in particular for the Catholic populace. After winning their war for independence in 1821, the Mexican government deported most of the Spanish Catholic clergy out of fear they would remain loyal to Spain. As a result, very few Catholic priests remained in the area, and they were the only ones with the authorization to administer the sacraments fundamental to the practice of Catholicism. This was especially true in the rural areas of what would become New Mexico and southern Colorado.

Although Penitentes probably existed in the Southwest for most of the long Spanish occupation, it is generally accepted that the Penitente society came to prominence after the Mexican War of Independence in 1821. The Penitente Brotherhood provided a way for Catholics without access to priests to share prayers and otherwise keep their Catholic faith alive. And remnants of their existence can still be found today.

Shortly after we became aware of Los Hermanos Penitentes, we discovered a morada, the building they use for their religious practices, near Grants, New Mexico, accompanied by an adjacent cemetery filled with old gravestones and cholla cactus. We returned occasionally to see it again, attracted to and entranced by its closed and lonesome feel.

We have since come across other moradas in northern New Mexico. We encountered two in the Abiquiú area, one that may still be in use and another reduced to adobe ruins beside a highway. A hand-painted sign in front of the highway ruins dates its construction to the year 1734.

Stories about Los Hermanos Penitentes sometimes focus on their historic practice of flagellation, and it may still exist in some places, but it is not unique to the brotherhood. Some clergy and members of the Catholic Church have engaged in flagellation, almost since Catholicism's founding, as a way to remember Christ's suffering. Members of the Franciscan Order were its best-known adherents, but others existed as well. Over the Church's long history flagellation was sometimes condemned, sometimes allowed, and often intentionally overlooked.

In his book *The Penitentes of New Mexico*, Ray John Aragón describes flagellation in New Mexico long before the Penitente Brotherhood arose:

> Penitential activities were introduced into New Mexico with the arrival of Don Juan de Oñate and his colonists in 1598. Under the spiritual guidance of Franciscan friars, the colonists observed Holy Week upon the banks of a small stream . . .
>
> The soldiers, with cruel scourges, beat their backs unmercifully until the camp ran crimson with their blood. . . . Don Juan . . . went to a secluded spot where he cruelly scourged himself, mingling bitter tears with the blood which ran from his many wounds. This continued throughout the camp until early morn.

To define today's Penitentes by flagellation, though, is to misunderstand their essence. They are people who practice their Catholic religion in the ways of their ancestors, sometimes while also attending a mainstream Catholic church. Through their services of mutual aid and charity they have long provided a vital supportive fabric to their communities.

When the Brotherhood became prominent in the Southwest in the nineteenth century, the Catholic Church denounced them, due in part to their physical penances. This drove them to worship in secret, and it wasn't until January 1947 that they were formally embraced as members of the Catholic faith. In his statement recognizing the Brotherhood, Archbishop Edwin D. Byrne of Santa Fe, New Mexico, acknowledged that they had preserved the Catholic faith during very difficult times, and he pledged to them his blessings and help.

One afternoon we attended a presentation at the Old School Gallery by Abe Peña, a man who had grown up in the 1930s and 1940s on a sheep ranch near the village of San Mateo, just a few miles from Grants, New Mexico. After Mr. Peña served in the Peace Corps and the United States Agency for International Development in several foreign countries, he moved back to San Mateo. There he wrote articles for the Grants newspaper *The Beacon* and several other publications, and he organized some of his writing into an informative book, *Memories of Cibola*, about which he came to speak to us.

Mr. Peña was an avuncular person and an excellent storyteller who loved to talk about his childhood experiences. He described attending services at the morada in San Mateo and said his family would also sometimes attend services at the Catholic church. During Holy Week he said they prayed the Stations of the Cross along with a nightly Rosary in the morada starting on Wednesday, when they locked themselves in until Holy Saturday, the day they were allowed to return home. Then on Easter Sunday they joined their Franciscan priest at the church to celebrate the Holy Eucharistic Mass of the Resurrection.

Penitente numbers have dwindled but they are still around, gathering in their small, windowless, two-room moradas. Most of their activities and ceremonies are similar to those of other Catholic groups, but with some significant differences in details. They have their own hymns called alabados, for instance, a Spanish word that means praise. Alabados are sung a capella by one or more voices, sometimes with occasional drumming or blowing of whistles, and many are ancient. They sound reminiscent of Gregorian chants and some even of Native American singing.

Today, Penitentes remain somewhat secretive. Perhaps, like many Native American religious groups who guard their practices, Penitentes remember their long history of suppression and wish to avoid the gawking of strangers. To honor their privacy I have not identified the specific locations of the moradas mentioned in this writing.

Much of the entrancement of northern New Mexico comes from its rich cultural mosaic, which certainly includes the Penitentes. A book of black-and-white photographs and text on the Penitente moradas of New Mexico titled *En Divina Luz*, by Craig Varjabedian and Michael Wallis, captures their atmospheric beauty and provides some examples of how Penitente practices and history are interwoven with those of other groups.

At one point the book describes a remote place at the end of a terraced field, in a tiny rural village in northern New Mexico, where ruins of a Tewa Pueblo lie beneath a Penitente morada constructed by Genízaros, who are descendants of Native slaves owned by the Spanish. The energies of these various peoples and cultures exist there together, untrammeled by the modern world.

27. Ramah Lake

THE INTERMITTENT ZUNI RIVER twists and turns down hillsides, tumbles through upper and lower waterfalls, and runs across the valley floor into Ramah Lake. The lake receives its primary recharge in the spring from the water the river collects from some 1,300 square miles of the Zuni Mountains, and the amount varies widely, depending mostly on melting winter snowpack.

As a result, the lake changes in size greatly from year to year and season to season. In a wet year it may extend up to two miles in length, and in a dry year it can dwindle to a small pond. The lake's maximum water depth was once ninety-five feet at the dam, but it has decreased significantly over time because of siltation.

Even during a drought a reserve pool of water almost always remains at the dam, but there have been a few years when the lake dried up completely. This happened a couple of times while we lived in the area, and during one of these years my grandson Silas and I used the opportunity to wander the dusty lake bed, looking for things revealed by the water's recession.

We discovered metal anchors, homemade anchors of cement-filled cans, a very nice filleting knife, old rods and reels, sunken row boats, shoes, and miscellaneous fishing tackle. One day we went out to the lake bed to explore and the wind and dust came up so hard that we had to stop and leave. It felt weird to be driven off the lake bed by a dust storm.

Because Ramah Lake lies at the end of a valley between two lines of bluffs, it is a narrow, curving body of water. To me it is most beautiful on summer mornings, just after dawn. On those days Dorn, who had built himself a workshop and house near the lake, Danny, who lives in Timberlake, and I would occasionally fish. We would gather early, stow our gear in Dorn's old aluminum boat, and push off into the still water.

Floating slowly around the edges and casting our wormed hooks and bobbers, we waited for a strike from a rainbow trout or bluegill. We might chat quietly about this or that, but mostly we drifted on the mirrored water, lost in the reflections of ponderosas, cottonwoods, bluffs, and sky.

For many years the New Mexico Fish and Game Department stocked the lake annually with rainbow trout, but that stopped when their agreement ended with the irrigation district that manages the water in the lake. There have been proposals over the years to expand the lake and revitalize the fishery by raising the dam, but because of the high cost and the state engineer's structural concerns, it has never occurred.

As a primary source of water in an arid landscape, Ramah Lake attracts a rich mix of wildlife. A pair of ospreys, large fish hawks, nested each year in the top of a ponderosa beside the lake, and they often fished while we did. They would soar high above the water, plummet like spears through the lake's surface, and emerge with their catch. Great blue herons stalked slowly in the shallows, a few nesting ducks and mud hens paddled about, and once I saw the only kingfisher I have ever seen, a brilliant flash of green as it dove and rose with a small fish in his bill.

Each year in spring a small flock of pelicans visited the lake, and Dorn, whose proximity to the lake made him its unofficial steward, would call us and a few others to let us know they had arrived. Because the pelicans only remained for a few days, we would promptly drive down to see them riding the choppy waves like a cluster of white bobbers.

No one knows precisely how long the lake has existed; there is some indication that the Navajo had a small dam there long before white people arrived. We do know that an early Mormon named Ernest Tietjen created the first modern dam with the help of twenty hired Navajo men, one yoke of oxen, and a scraper made from Fort Wingate scrap. Since 1880 the dam has washed out and been rebuilt three or four times. It has also been improved and maintained over the years, sometimes at heroic expense and labor by the people in Ramah, who use the water for irrigation.

The land beside and beneath one end of the lake is owned by the Timberlake Homeowners Association, and the other end is public property. We would occasionally see kayakers or canoers, and once in a while folks fishing from a boat or the bank, but most days the lake was unoccupied.

We often walked the roads that ran along both sides; each offers very different landscapes and views. Sometimes we clambered up the cliffs that line the lake to access the vistas that opened wider and wider as we went up. We enjoyed walking and climbing there without another person present, as if we had our own private park. El Morro National Monument felt the same way; although it received much more foot traffic than Ramah Lake, our strolls along its trails, especially in winter, were often alone. We were very grateful for these two places, which we thought of as our backyards.

Once, during his annual visit, my son Adam brought along a drone he had built, and on a late afternoon we flew it from the Timberlake ranch house toward the lake. As it soared through the dusk along the lakeshore, the controller suddenly stopped working and we watched in dismay as the drone continued its flight away and finally dropped in the twilight. We thought we had a good idea where it landed, but we searched for it unsuccessfully until dark made us stop.

We looked for it again the next day, along the shore and up the hillsides, through brush and rock-filled arroyos, and even along the opposite shore, until we had to give up. I felt bad about Adam's loss of something he spent so long assembling, but he took it in stride. "I'll just build a better one," he said. "I know what happened, and how to keep it from happening again." I think of the drone resting on the lake bottom until, in a dry year, its discovery surprises some other father and son.

One of our most personal connections to the lake occurred a couple of years later, after Matt passed away. Matt was a serious amateur photographer and felt especially drawn to the colors and shapes of the New Mexico sky and landscape. When he was home in Virginia he would sometimes call for his sons or his wife, Eed, saying, "Come and look at the clouds. It's like a New Mexico sky out here."

We held a gathering for Matt beside Ramah Lake, one of his favorite places to photograph, attended by our family and many of the people out there who had gotten to know him. Roger, who is a Buddhist cleric, led the ceremony, and Jon and Pam bravely paddled their flower-garlanded kayaks out into the lake against a strong wind and released some of Matt's ashes into the water. We also scattered his ashes on the land that his brother, Tim, owns, which overlooks the lake. Then we gathered at our friend Dana's house to share memories and a potluck dinner.

After we moved to Albuquerque we took a trip to Thailand, a gift from Matt's wife, Eed, who is Thai. She called us one day and said, "Matt and I always wanted to take you to Thailand, and I would love to do it now." While there we scattered some of his ashes in the Mekong, a river that held special significance to him.

Matt's ashes now grace two bodies of water he loved, half a world apart.

Five years after Matt's death my son, Adam, died, and we wove another thread of deep connection to Ramah Lake as we released a bit of his ashes into it and interred the rest in the nearby countryside.

28. Water Wars

RURAL LIFE CONTAINS ABUNDANT blessings. Ours did. A home surrounded by natural beauty and a caring community drew and held us for many years. But country living also has its challenges, and one of the foremost is the lack of municipal services, especially water. Many rural houses need a well, and sooner or later water security will top a homeowner's worry list.

It might happen like this: A couple from Phoenix or Dallas or Baltimore seeks refuge from the clamor of megalopolis in the serenity of a country home. They hear about our area, make a visit, and stop by the Inscription Rock Trading and Coffee Company. After meeting a few friendly and interesting folks and wandering over to the Ancient Way Café where they encounter more of the same, they hike the trail up to the top of El Morro National Monument. While looking out across the sunflower-covered valley they become hooked. This is the place for them.

They can't believe how cheap the land is, five or ten acres for a fraction of the cost of a tiny lot in a big city, so they purchase a parcel, and for their next step they must make sure they have access to water. After asking around they find that there are three or four well drillers available, but no consensus as to who is best.

Each driller has people who hold them in regard, but others who wouldn't hire them on a bet. They talk to a couple of drillers, pick one, and sign them up.

The driller sets up their rig and starts drilling, a process that could go on for several days, depending on how deep they have to go. They will probably hit water, but it could be low flow or saline. The hope is for a well with good water that is deep enough; a shallow well could fail in dry years. But too deep isn't good either, because the cost rises for each foot the drill goes down.

The owners might follow the progress from their city home or decide to rent a local motel room and sit in lawn chairs all day, watching as the drill slowly turns. Whether or not they hit water, it will cost them thousands of dollars. If they don't get a good well, the driller might offer to try again in a different spot for a lower price.

Hopefully they do get good water and can build their home and settle in, but their well will always be a small concern that niggles in the backs of their minds. Then comes the almost inevitable day when they turn on the tap and no water pours out, and their worry flares.

Maybe it's nothing, just a circuit breaker that needs to be reset, but maybe it's the worst: the well has gone dry. It could be a failed pump or a lightning strike that burned out the electronics (which happened to us), or something else requiring expert attention. In any case, they don't flush the toilets because the driller they called for repairs might not show up right away.

The bottom line is that rural people tend to be very sensitive to anything that might threaten their wells. That's why folks got so upset in early 2001, when they received a legal document in the mail from the US Department of Justice telling them that they and all the other well owners in the area were being sued by the federal government, the State of New Mexico, and the Zuni and Navajo Tribes. The lawsuit, called the Zuni River Basin Water Rights Adjudication, was initiated to define and quantify all rights to surface and groundwater in the drainage basin of the Zuni River, which included where they lived. One word in the letter, "defendant," really jumped out at them. They were defendants in a federal lawsuit!

They immediately imagined having to spend big money on a lawyer and their anxiety shot up a whole bunch of notches. The worst part, though, was that the federal government wanted a court to declare that tribal water rights have priority over everybody else's. "Oh my god," people thought. "The feds and Zuni and Navajo are trying to shut down my well!"

A little background about water rights might be useful here. In the eastern part of the United States, where water is generally abundant, riparian water rights prevail. Under this system all owners of land adjacent to bodies of water have the right to make reasonable use of them. In the West, however, where water is scarce, the dominant rule is prior appropriation, which means that people who began using a particular water source earlier have rights over those who come along and use it later.

In other words, if the court agreed with the Justice Department that "tribal rights to water under or on Indian land have priority over any other rights because they have existed for time immemorial," and also determined that the use of domestic wells interfered with tribal water use, domestic wells in the area might be metered, limited, or even closed.

The Justice Department and the state eventually held meetings to try to bring calm to the situation, but because people were already so angry and didn't trust what was being said, their efforts proved ineffective. We remember one public meeting at El Morro National Monument where a few of the attendees in the standing room–only crowd completely ignored and shouted down the government representatives. They weren't there to listen; they had come to express their anger and opposition.

After several months the part of the suit that affected homeowners was laid to rest, and almost all domestic well owners were issued court orders giving them rights to seven-tenths of an acre-foot per year of water. This is a very large amount of water, enough to cover an entire acre of land to a depth of seven-tenths of a foot. The rest of the lawsuit is a tussle between tribes and big water users such as municipalities, utility companies, and mines. These are very complicated issues, and the litigation involving them will probably go on for many years.

In the long run the process will provide good results for most everyone. Well water rights will be more secure because court decrees will specifically define them. Also, the future of water availability in the area will be brighter because large water users will have a harder time coming in and depleting the resource.

Beyond the issue of well water rights, an additional aspect of the litigation concerned us, which involved the security of Ramah Lake. The lake is an asset to New Mexico, a biological and recreational treasure. Unfortunately, though, its dam impedes the river that flows to the Zuni Reservation. Also, because New Mexico law only protects water used by people, there is no place in the allocation process for preserving the water's scenic and ecological value.

We wrote Governor Richardson in 2007 and asked for help with this issue. Among other things, we requested that he direct someone from one of the state agencies, perhaps the Environment Department or the Department of Game and Fish, to participate in the water allocation process and speak for the protection of the lake as a natural resource. We also sent similar letters to the heads of state agencies, members of the state legislature, and others, but we were dismayed by the lack of response we received. We got no response from anyone.

Water rights have long been among the most contentious subjects in the Southwest. We knew two couples in the Ramah area who shared a well and got so mad at each other over it that they fired rifles at each other's houses. John Nichols's classic novel, *The Great Milagro Beanfield War*, and the movie based on it that starred Robert Redford, dramatize beautifully just what a fighting word "water" can be out here.

29. Big Bird and Little Bird

IF THE RAMAH AREA had a spirit animal, it would be the common raven. Ravens are bigger than life and have character that demands attention. Other animals, such as cougars, bears, and elk, also have a strong presence in the area, but they rarely engage with humans. No other New Mexico denizen is as playful, intelligent, or ubiquitous as the raven.

In addition to the common raven, which inhabits the entire state, Chihuahuan ravens reside in southern New Mexico, but they are smaller, more crow-like, and carry considerably less presence.

The raven is a big brother to the crow. Crows are the size of pigeons, and ravens are 50 percent larger—almost as big as red-tail hawks. Crows mostly caw, while ravens make all kinds of noises, the most common being a low, raspy croak. Both birds are members of the corvid family, which also includes jays and magpies. All the corvids are brash and smart—the Einstein mafiosi of the bird world. Although ravens and crows exist throughout the state, we mostly saw ravens while in Ramah.

Both crows and ravens can imitate sounds, including the human voice. I have heard that some people who kept crows as pets incorrectly believed they could only pronounce words if their tongues were slit, but I never met anyone who has seen or carried out such a cruel operation.

Ravens are slightly more intelligent than crows and definitely more acrobatic in flight, but in many ways the two species are very much alike. Both mate for life, have phenomenal memories and problem-solving skills, and are very playful. And some of what has been discovered about them is almost unbelievable. They don't only use tools they find, for example, they can construct them. Given a wire, a raven can figure out how to bend it into a hook and use the hook to pull food out of a bottle.

In some locales the birds have learned to drop nuts onto busy streets so cars crack them open, and they may even select intersections with streetlights so they can get at the nutmeats safely while the light is red. They have been observed dropping bread on water to attract fish; working together to distract predators so others can steal their food; and pointing with their beaks, just as we point with our fingers, to direct each other's attention. In some activities, such as task planning, ravens are even smarter than apes, so if someone calls you a bird brain, smile and thank them for the compliment.

Ravens play keep-away, follow-the-leader, and king of the mountain. They slide down snowy roofs, hang upside down from branches, and perform exuberant dances in the sky. Loop-the-loop, soar and drop, and tumble are standard maneuvers in their aerial display, and most of it seems to be just for fun. Especially in the spring, when they dance in the air with their mate, their performances can be quite impressive and entertaining.

Our day would brighten a bit when we spotted a raven or two sitting on top of a tall dead tree or watched as they strutted on the ground. Sometimes, especially when walking through a forested area, the whoosh of their large wings would startle us as they passed closely overhead. We became attached to the ones that hung around our house and let each other know when we spotted them.

A neighbor had a pair of ravens that stayed near her house so they could grab scraps she regularly put out for them in her yard. They eat almost anything and cache the leftover food for a later meal. Juicy bits of a carcass, for example, may be hidden in several different places. The people who worked at El Morro National Monument would let us know when the same pair of ravens that nested next to the visitor center year after year had chicks and when the parent birds finally pushed their young out to learn to fly. People who have raised ravens as pets discover that they are complex, loyal, and demanding.

In their mafioso way, ravens and crows can take umbrage and remember their enemies for a long time. Our friends Reed and Fran had a pair of them that nested nearby, and, for some reason, the ravens decided this friendly, nature-loving couple were their enemies. The birds embarked on a reign of terror, pulling the rubber out of their windshield wipers, tearing the rubber seals out of their sliding doors, and dive-bombing and vocally harassing their dog. To our friends' relief the aggressive behavior died away fairly quickly, though they never told us whether acquiescence to raven extortion was involved

Crows and ravens can both carry long grudges, particularly against people who capture and release them for scientific purposes. The birds recognize and recall the faces of individuals for years and will follow and scold them with raucous cries. Students at the University of Washington who conduct crow studies wear masks when trapping and working with the birds so they won't be hounded by them later as they walk across the campus.

The pygmy nuthatch, a tiny songbird with a short tail, gray back, white front, and nut-brown cap, is at the other end of the size spectrum. We had other nuthatches in our area, but I especially like the pygmy because it is cuter and packs a lot of attitude in a very small body.

Of my favorite memories of pygmy nuthatches, I particularly

recall the sounds of their companionable chatter and tapping on the branches that covered our ramada when we sat under it in the morning with our coffee. I enjoyed watching them walk easily up and down the trunks of trees as if they were on level ground and pound tree bark like woodpeckers (which they are not). When they pound at trees they are usually cracking open seeds they stuck in bark crevices to get at the nutmeats.

Pygmy nuthatches are fairly fearless of humans and sometimes chittered at us as if to scold. They got particularly put out when I let the bird feeders in the yard remain empty too long. It felt really strange to be bullied by something as tiny and appealing as a pygmy nuthatch.

30. Bear Heart

MARCELLUS "BEAR HEART" WILLIAMS was not a large man, but his presence and deep voice filled a room. All kinds of people sought him out, drawn to his simple, caring messages distilled from a lifetime of exploration and experience. We first met him and Reginah, his medicine helper who became his wife, at the wedding we attended when we first moved to Ramah. Then we ran into them a few times in our area over the years, usually when Bear Heart was officiating at another wedding or a funeral.

Bear Heart was born in 1918 in Okemah, Oklahoma, into the Muskogee Nation Creek Tribe. He learned traditional tribal medicine from his uncles, and his mother steeped him in the Christian faith. He had an undergraduate degree and a divinity degree, became an ordained Baptist minister, and led ceremonies as a roadman in the Native American Church. The varieties and commonalities of religions and belief systems of the world were for Bear Heart a lifelong fascination.

Because the Native American Church contains a blend of Indian and Christian traditions it was a natural fit for Bear Heart. The church was founded by a man named Quanah Parker, who was born around 1850 in eastern Texas to a Comanche father and an

Anglo mother. William T. Hagan, in his book *Quanah Parker, Comanche Chief*, describes the Native American Church this way: "Elements of Christianity were melded with the original Native features. Quanah himself described the peyote-centered worship, declaring, 'The white man goes into his church house and talks about Jesus, but the Indian goes into his tipi and talks to Jesus.'"

A Native American Church service is usually held in a teepee or sweat lodge over an entire night, and participants eat peyote and drink peyote tea. Peyote is a small cactus containing a psychoactive drug called mescaline, which has long been used as medicine and in rituals by Native Americans. Although federal law classifies it as an illegal drug, its use by the Native American Church has been legislatively and judicially affirmed by statutes in twenty-eight states, the Federal Religious Freedom Restoration Act of 1993, the Oregon State Supreme Court, and the US Supreme Court.

Leaders of the services are called roadmen, not because they travel from place to place but because they help members stay on the right road of life. One of the most influential early Native American Church roadmen was a Delaware religious leader named John Wilson, a direct ancestor of Father John. It's interesting how these three seemingly unconnected people—Bear Heart, Joy Harjo, and Father John—are threaded together by birth and circumstance.

Bear Heart's history includes praying with President Truman in the Oval Office, providing spiritual counseling to rescue workers and their families after the 1995 Oklahoma City tragedy, and praying with firefighters at Ground Zero in New York City after the destruction of the World Trade Center on September 11, 2001. He led vision quests all over the country, and people from around the world traveled to New Mexico to sit and confer with him.

One day, when Bear Heart and Reginah were staying with us, Bear Heart asked me if I would like to accompany him while he performed a medicine ceremony for a friend suffering from breast cancer. I told him I would be honored. We drove to her house, and

Bear Heart received her permission for me to be present. I sat in the background and watched as he whispered to her, chanted, sang in his Native language, and fanned tobacco smoke across her body.

Afterward, on our way back home, Bear Heart told me that he did not heal people; only the Creator has that ability. His work, including its ceremonies and spiritual trappings, helped folks open themselves to the possibility of healing. He also mentioned that there is a tradition among medicine people to pass on their skills and knowledge by teaching apprentices, and he sometimes wished that he had an apprentice who would carry on his work after he was gone.

When Bear Heart died he did not have an apprentice, but he did leave a rich legacy. He had given his fireplace (taught his way as a roadman in the Native American Church) to several other roadmen, and some vision quest presenters continue to lead quests in his manner. He enhanced the lives of many people through his voice and presence, and his teachings continue to be shared through his printed words and videos of his talks and ceremonies. Bear Heart was a man with not just one apprentice but a multiplicity of people carrying on his ways, and that's about as good as it gets.

Bear Heart's counsel covers a wide gamut of personal, spiritual, and societal subjects. One issue he decried, for example, was the paucity of rites of passage in modern life. He would point to the Jewish Bar and Bat Mitzvah coming-of-age celebrations as among the few that remain. Also, some Native cultures still hold ceremonies to mark life changes, such as the ones held for soldiers returning from war to help them find their place in society again. A rite that honors a soldier's service, acknowledges their need to heal, and welcomes them back home can go a long way toward easing his or her reentry.

I especially like Bear Heart's take on leadership. He said that traditionally, the chief was the poorest man in the tribe. If he went on a hunt and brought back game, he gave it to widows who could not hunt for themselves. He existed to serve the people and he did it without resentment and with a sense of duty. When people lined up to eat, the chief stayed in the back and let others eat first. You don't see that today, he remarked. Now the leaders are always the first to eat.

That didn't mean, he added, we should return completely to the old traditions, but our societies would function better if our leaders lived in ways of service that earned the respect of the people.

I saw this in action while working for EPA when I attended a national conference on Indian environmental law on the Cherokee Reservation near Ashville, North Carolina. I stood in the back of the meeting room the first morning with a few other early arrivals, watching a man in work clothes set up tables and chairs. When I asked the person next to me a question about the reservation, he pointed to the man setting up the room and said, "I don't know, ask him—he's the chief."

One aspect of Bear Heart's teachings that made them so widely accepted was his broad inclusiveness. He referred to people from many ethnic backgrounds and walks of life as his nephews, nieces, children, and grandchildren. Although he had no cultural relations to many of these folks, he welcomed them all into his extended family. The groom at the wedding in the woods and another young man whose funeral he performed in our area, for example, carried no apparent Native American identity but still called him grandfather. To Bear Heart we were all family, and this reflected in not just what he said but in how he lived.

Bear Heart understood that the greatest value of tribal membership is shared culture, and the greatest cost is when it becomes an excuse to make war with and take from others. He honored his tribe for its culture, but he also cared for all people as members with him of the great human tribe.

31. Sun Dance

MANY YEARS AGO WE watched a movie titled *A Man Called Horse*, starring Richard Harris, who portrayed an Englishman captured by the Sioux. In order to become a member of the tribe he was required to undergo a sun dance that included piercing both sides of his chest. That movie was on our minds when we attended a sun dance as guests of Bear Heart and Reginah.

Sun dances are one of the most traditional and important ceremonies performed by Plains Indian tribes in both Canada and the United States. They and some other Native ceremonies were illegal for many years due to negative stereotyping and the belief that Indigenous people should be forced away from their cultures and into the Eurocentric mainstream. The prohibition was eventually lifted in Canada in 1951, and in the United States in 1978, when the American Indian Religious Freedom Act was passed.

Although they share commonalities, Native sun dance traditions differ. Some, for example, include piercings, while others don't. Some take place within a structure, while others are conducted under the open sky. They all, however, involve self-sacrificial acts that include, among other practices, long periods of dancing without food or drink.

Our sun dance experience with Bear Heart and Reginah occurred in July 2005, when they stayed with us while participating in one near the Ramah Navajo Reservation. They invited us to accompany them because they knew of our interest and thought the experience would help me as I edited Bear Heart's second book, *The Bear Is My Father*.

They arrived at our house late one afternoon and attended the dance for most of the next four days. Bear Heart had sun danced eight times during his life, and at this dance he would be an honored elder and grandfather. He would talk to the dancers before they began and provide spiritual support and his medicine when needed.

If we lingered at home too long in the mornings, Bear Heart wouldn't say anything; he'd just put on his hat, pick up his stick, and, even though the dance grounds were twenty miles away, start walking down the road. When Reginah noticed he was gone she'd get in the car and pick him up wherever he had gotten to, and they'd be on their way.

On the first day we followed their car down the highway until we came to a rutted dirt road that wove through ponderosas and piñons and led to a cluster of tents and small trailers where we parked. After a walk past two sweat lodges and a large fire pit with a half dozen bison skulls on its rim, we arrived at the dance circle.

A group of Oglala Lakota from the Pine Ridge Reservation conducted this ceremony, and their tradition includes piercing and dancing outside under the sun. This was the third year the dance had been held at this place, which would host one more. We were told that these sun dances were usually held annually in one location for four years, after which a new location was selected to restart the cycle.

Although this spot had already hosted for the two prior years, everything had to be set up anew. Cooking and restroom facilities were brought in, and the dancing circle was completely reconstructed. Of primary importance was the selection and placement of the tall tree in the center of the dance circle.

A ring of sunshades made of branches and plastic sheets to shelter observers, drummers, and singers surrounded the dance area. Another ring of upright sticks marked the line between the inner dance circle and the outer circle of sunshades. At the very center of the dance circle stood the tree, an enormous cottonwood that had been felled with ceremony the previous day, then transported to the site and anchored in the ground.

The tree stood sixty feet tall, straight and smooth except for its upper reaches, where branches and green leaves rustled in the hot July wind. Several ropes hung from the top, their lower ends tied loosely to the tree's base. Long pieces of bright prayer cloth hung down from the high branches, and a horizontal bundle of sticks was tied three-quarters of the way up the tree. We later learned that the bundle contained branches from the tree that had centered the last year's dance.

Reginah and Bear Heart found their place among the elders, and we set up our chairs under the sunshade with the other guests, most of whom were family and friends there to support the dancers. Reginah had told us to remove our hats and refrain from eating or drinking while in the circle. We didn't wear hats because it would dishonor the dancers who danced with bare heads in the sun, and we didn't eat or drink because it would be disrespectful of the dancers' fasts. We arrived after the dances had begun; the next dance would be the first to involve piercing.

Before the next dance began a buffalo robe was carried to the base of the tree and spread out. Four of the ropes hanging from the top of the tree were stretched out, one in each direction, and fastened to stakes in the ground. Then the drummers and singers settled around an enormous drum and began the rhythmic thump and repetitive song that would continue throughout every dance for all four days.

The dancers, who numbered about forty, were given a talk by Bear Heart before they entered the circle. Their ages varied; a surprising number appeared to be in their fifties or sixties. Then they took their places and began shuffling clockwise around the tree.

The men were bare-chested and mostly barefoot, although a few wore moccasins. They wore straight skirts of red material, with green, woven circlets on their heads. The women wore dresses or skirts of various colors and simple tops or blouses. They would dance each day for six hours beneath the intense July sun without food or water.

Occasionally, a couple of bare-chested, young Native men with long black hair circulated with forked sticks that held large aluminum cans filled with coals. They scattered sage, an aromatic herb used in many tribal ceremonies, on the coals and held the cans out to the dancers or passed them around the base of the tree or the buffalo skulls. They also moved among the guests so each person could bend over the cans and pull the fragrant smoke over their heads. Their presence throughout all four days provided a continuous blessing and cleansing.

Three members of the gay community in our area also danced vigorously around the perimeter of the circle, wherever their spirits took them. They were also there for the entire ceremony, shaking rattles and feather fans, lending energy and support.

A man wearing a buffalo headdress moved around the periphery, snapping a whip, grinning at children, and being a leavening influence. I later learned that he was a buffalo dancer and, like the Zuni mudheads, functioned as a clown whose duty was to lighten the mood, bring a spot of humor, and gently keep everyone on the right path.

During the dances we guests stood and shuffled from foot to foot with the long, repetitious rhythm of the drum. As the dancers circled the tree we gradually faded into the spirit of it all.

Four people were pierced in that dance, and a few more in each dance thereafter. Not all the dancers, however, had chosen to be pierced. Piercing for men involved cutting slits and inserting small wooden dowels beneath the skin on either side of the chest.

Piercing for women was similar, except that it was done on the outside of the upper arms just below the shoulders.

The men were laid on the buffalo robe at the base of the tree for their piercing, and the women were pierced while they stood. Then each of the four was led to one of the ropes stretched out to a stake in the ground.

The ropes were removed from the stakes and looped over the dowels under the dancers' skin, tethering them to the tree. The tethered dancers moved in place, facing the tree with the ropes loosely stretched out and up, while the other dancers continued to circle behind them. Eventually, after a series of movements toward the tree and back out, the tethered dancers lunged backward against the ropes and broke free.

When people who had danced in the hot July sun for hours or days without food or water finally pulled the dowels through their skin and collapsed into the arms of their supporters, everyone, including the guests, experienced their release. Finally, as each dance ended, the dancers moved from the circle, turning with raised hands as they came out. Then the drum and singers fell silent.

That day we witnessed several dances, until one dance in the late afternoon seemed to stretch on forever in the scorching sun. The temperature was in the low nineties, we were at 7,200 feet above sea level, and the dancers had gone the whole day without food or drink. Then, as if the earth itself suddenly decided the dance had gone on long enough, the sky became gray, a slight rain began, and a gale arose that drove dust into all our eyes and tore down some of the sunshades and the wooden structures to which they were attached.

The dance quickly ended as the wind pushed the dancers out of the circle. At that point we had been there for about six hours, and we decided to leave. There would be one more dance, but we were tired, so we walked to our car and drove home.

Bear Heart and Reginah attended all the dances on each of the days, and I returned by myself two days later. I had forgotten to bring a chair, so I settled onto a blanket next to a friend who had arrived earlier and waited. Eventually, the drummers and singers began their music, and the dancers moved in. We observers began shuffling in place to the beat, while the support dancers moved along the sides and the cedar men circled with their aromatic smoke.

We stood, watching and moving rhythmically to the drum, and again melded into the powerful process. The dancers in front of us partook in an ancient practice rooted in the culture of the Plains Indians and in the earth itself. They danced for spiritual reasons, their efforts requiring an enormous amount of focus and self-discipline. We were honored to be, in a small way, part of it all.

Each evening, when Bear Heart and Reginah returned to our house, Bear Heart was full of energy. This surprised us, given his age and his strenuous days at the dance. Reginah told us that throughout the nights he kept her awake by praying softly.

As we prepared dinner he would sit in the living room and read a mystery novel with a plate of cheese and crackers, and the rest of us would gather in the kitchen and talk until the food was ready. During our supper we asked Bear Heart questions about this and that, mostly about the sun dance itself. He responded that before the first dance began he met with the dancers and sang the sun dance song he had received from his brother Black Elk. Then he told them that he himself had sun danced eight times, so he knew their sacrifices, what was in their hearts and minds. He said to them that they would be tempted and tested in ways that would strengthen their inner beings, helping them make their sacrifices and express their love for their life, for the people around them, and for the earth that sustains us all.

"Before the European influence of religion, our Native teaching was that to be blessed in a good way, you have to suffer," he explained. "The first teaching of Buddhism is that all life is a struggle. We appreciate and acknowledge every day the life that is given to us and say thank you for giving us another day."

I asked Bear Heart why people perform the sun dance, and he answered that each dancer has their own personal motives. They might dance for a sick relative or friend. Perhaps they sought answer to a question such as what path they should take in their life, or maybe they just wanted to express their love of Mother Earth. There are as many different reasons for dancing the sun dance as there are dancers.

As I researched the sun dance, I discovered what seem to be two opposing attitudes expressed among Native Americans. Some believe the dance should remain a private ceremony, with participation restricted to those of Indian blood. This protectiveness is based in part on the historical repression of Native religious practices in this country and the fact that this ceremony in particular was once condemned by law as barbaric. Additionally, there is a concern that making the sun dance more widely available to non-participants and non-Natives dilutes its sanctity.

Other people think access to the ceremony should be more widely available, as inspiration to both Native peoples and others who may not have the opportunity or be allowed to attend or participate. Also, for the sun dance to not disappear like so many other Native cultural practices, it needs an existence beyond those few who can experience it directly.

Whatever happens, Lucia and I are grateful that we were allowed to be present for such an ancient and powerful expression of love for and connection to our mother, the earth.

32. Sueños

EXPERIENCES IN LOCALES THAT carry a strong sense of place may be shaded with a whiff of mystery, a touch of awe. I remember one night when this felt especially true.

Eight of us had gathered with Pam, Jon, and their son, Walker, at their place, the Inscription Rock Trading and Coffee Company in El Morroville, for dinner. As dusk faded into night, we sat and chatted around a table on the patio beside the store.

Behind us stood the huge mesa. Small lights hung in the piñons and junipers at the edges of the patio, rows of votive candles flickered on the table in the light breeze, and above us stretched the starry sky. We guests were people who, like our hosts, had moved to the area from other parts of the country, and all of us had rooted here and become good friends.

We had finished a fine meal of tamales, frijoles, calabacitas, and salad, and we relaxed into our chairs sipping sherry or port as we drifted on soft murmurs of conversation. Jon talked about the events of the prior weekend and a concert that Tony had performed at the Old School Gallery, just across the highway from where we sat. Tony was a guitarist and singer who lived in the area, and he was going to Europe to get married.

During the last song of Tony's concert, a blend of "Somewhere over the Rainbow" and "What a Wonderful World," Jon had played along on the charango, an Andean stringed instrument, something like a small mandolin but sweeter in sound. It has a rounded wooden back that in earlier times would have been made from an armadillo shell. Its strings are arranged in pairs, with each pair tuned together, except for one set that is tuned an octave apart.

As we sat there in the comfort of that July evening, Jon talked about how special Tony's last performance was to him, and how much he enjoyed playing the charango. Then he shifted his discussion to the day after Tony's concert when a group of Zuni men had come into the store and asked where they could find a particular type of tree whose boughs they needed for the rain dances that would be performed in their pueblo the next day.

Jon pointed them toward a gravel road that meandered across the Zuni Mountains, and a few hours later they returned to the store with their truck full of alligator juniper branches. They thanked Jon and Pam and left, buoyed by the blessings of their ancestors, whose spirits rode with the men now that they completed their gathering.

The experience had started Jon thinking about a conversation he and Pam had a few days earlier about people they met in dreams, people they knew during the dream who became strangers when they awakened. They wondered if those folks might be ancestors, people from previous lives, or strangers from somewhere else. Later that night, as he pondered the dream people and the blessings of his Zuni friends' ancestors, he began noodling on the charango, and a song emerged.

We all asked to hear the song and, with a little coaxing, Jon got out his charango and sang. The song was called "Sueños," the Spanish word for dreams, and it reflected on the folks that we meet in dreams who lovingly lay their hands on our shoulders or give us a smile or a gentle word. As we listened to Jon's soft voice, cocooned in the ease of that late evening, I know we all felt like the most fortunate people in the world. Because of times like these some of us who later moved away refer to ourselves as expats. The Ramah area was our homeland, our querencia.

Memories of old friends together, as we were that evening, are among the strongest evocations for me, and sensory memories such as smells can especially take us back. The fragrances hidden in the folds of ponderosa bark, for instance, were something we often shared with guests. We would tell them to put their nose against a large ponderosa tree and see whether they encountered the scent of vanilla or caramel. They'd look at us as if we were nuts and then laugh as they discovered the sweet, surprisingly similar smells.

Wood smoke remains particularly memory laden. On many evenings we sat with guests around the stone fire pit on our patio, chatting quietly amid the glow and fragrance of wood smoke while we watched bats dance through the wavering light. If the grandkids were there, we roasted marshmallows, mashing them between graham crackers and chocolate into s'mores. In my mind I can still call up the pungent, smoky aroma that enveloped me when the wind shifted my way and how my clothes carried it into the house.

I also remember so well driving through the dusk with the windows down just after a late summer shower and being transported by the sharp incense of wet sagebrush. It reminded me of the smell of the sage that grew along Montana streams where I fly-fished with my father. Then there was the stench of stinkbugs, the odd essence of sweet sand verbena, and the sour smell of wet burned wood permeating areas of extinguished forest fires.

Sometimes, too, a sight that suddenly jerks us out of the mundane can stick strongly in our memory. One year we attended the Red, Green, and Blues Festival in El Morroville, an annual Labor Day celebration of food and music that included a chile cook-off. After dinner we rocked to the blues music of Jon Pickens and his band, the Billyhawks. We were all looking forward to an evening under the stars, but it had rained off and on throughout the day, so the show was moved from the stage beside the Pickens' store into the Old School Gallery across the street.

The band was hot, and the old schoolhouse rocked to their blues and the bounce of the dancers. Finally, at about 10:30 p.m., we drove toward home, tired, full of chili, and stoked on the music. We had traveled down the dark highway, turned onto the gravel of Timberlake Road, and were curving through the valley toward our house.

Just past the old corrals and before the spread where an old Navajo man, Mr. Pino, had his fields and sheep, Lucia said, "What's that?" and pointed out the window. I glanced where she pointed, then slowly moved the car to the edge of the road and stopped. We sat there transfixed, staring at a tall, yellow light at the top of a mesa. As it shone, bright and motionless against the black sky, I first thought that it was some strange manifestation of the moon. This wasn't possible, though; the sky was filled with clouds, and the moon was in its dark phase.

Then it gradually dawned on us: We were seeing a single tree engulfed in flame, burning in the quiet air. We sat there stock-still; we'd never seen anything like it. Our mundane drive home had just flashed us into an otherworldly experience.

As we came to ourselves and got back on the road, we noticed two cars parked around the curve ahead with a couple of Zuni tribal policemen leaning against them. We pulled over and got out, and they told us the tree had been struck by lightning. They had called it in and the firefighters would soon arrive to climb up the hillside with their axes and shovels and put it out.

I have a bunch of such memories, all tucked away in a special cupboard in my mind: an October hayride that ended in a late-night circle of us singing softly together around a fire; the sudden appearance of a group of elk grazing just outside our living room windows; stepping out of a meeting in El Morroville to a sunset that made the sky appear on fire. Each is as bright as a new penny, and each carries me home.

33. Zuni Mountain Stupa

NEAR THE CONTINENTAL DIVIDE a gravel road runs north from Highway 53 for several miles up into the Zuni Mountains, then intersects a lane that curves into a wide meadow. There a bright, white stupa stands, thirty-four feet square and fifty feet tall, and no matter how many times we visit, the sight of it is always a startling incongruity: an imposing Tibetan Buddhist monument shining away in that remote New Mexico meadow.

As we pulled under a tree and got out of the car, Stan and Shirley walked into sight, smiling greetings. They looked like they belonged there—a genial, middle-aged couple in jeans who had lived on that land for decades. Then they blew their cover when they donated a piece of their property to a Buddhist foundation for the stupa, the last great work of Bhakha Tulku Rinpoche, the tenth reincarnation of a highly venerated Buddha master. He is referred to with the honorific of rinpoche, a Buddhist term for lamas, teachers, and abbots who carry great respect.

The stupa is in the shape of a white domed cube, upon which sits a white rectangle with stylized eyes. Atop it rests a tapered, gold crown. In front, a set of steps leads to a pair of tall, carved wooden doors that open into a square, high-ceilinged room. The interior houses rugs, bright-colored paintings, and an ornate throne flanked by seats on a dais at the back. Pillows lie around the floor, and a carved, wooden shrine runs along one wall.

Unlike Christian churches, Muslim mosques, and Jewish synagogues, Buddhist stupa interiors are not used for regular communal ceremonies or rituals. Stupas are religious monuments built as places for meditation, and they provide specific and general blessings to the earth and all beings upon it.

A circular walkway surrounds the outside of the stupa, and four life-size bronze Buddhas stand beneath wooden shelters along its path. A small stream flows down a hillside into a rock-lined pool, and bright, multi-colored prayer flags flutter near and far. You can spot some of the flags in the tops of tall pine trees; Shirley told us a tree-climbing monk visited on occasion and placed them there. She explained that the wooden buildings tucked among the trees behind the stupa serve as places for teachings, retreats, sleeping, dining, and cooking.

The external form of the stupa represents the meditating Buddha, and the essence of its making is intense spiritual focus and symbolism. A stupa is first created spiritually through prayer and ceremony, then constructed physically, following exact processes and forms that have existed for hundreds of years. Within the dome and the structure above it that holds the crown are millions of sacred objects: an entire library of Buddhist texts, millions of mantras, twenty-five thousand small statues of deities, and relics and other objects collected by Bhakha Tulku over his lifetime.

Construction was a joint effort, funded by numerous donations of money, materials, labor, and art from Buddhists and non-Buddhists. The carved wooden doors were created and donated by Charlie, a local artist and organic rancher, and the life-sized bronze statues were gifts from a group of Buddhists in California.

Shirley wrote an excellent book, titled *Building the Zuni Mountain Stupa*, in which she details its creation and significance and provides color photos throughout the text to bring it all to life. It is astonishing how a few people in that fairly inaccessible location could mobilize enough resources, volunteers, and creative experts to construct an exactly defined building of such beauty and complexity.

The particular purpose of this stupa, as Shirley's book explains, is "to subdue negativity and obstacles, bring harmony and balance to the environment, and alleviate the suffering of all beings—with a special focus on the plight of Native Americans." This special focus on the plight of Native Americans firmly weaves the stupa's blessings into the energy of the area.

Some might wonder why non-Buddhists would contribute to the building and operation of a stupa, but you don't have to be Buddhist to experience and appreciate what the religion has to offer. The Zuni Mountain Stupa provides blessings to everybody. This is a unique aspect of Buddhism—it doesn't require commitment to a system of beliefs before conferring its blessings. Just walking the circular path around the stupa base, for example, is said to bring purification and recovery from problems, especially if done at least three times. Before our visit a man had spent several days there circumambulating the stupa ten thousand times.

Shirley and Stan made great commitments to the stupa's creation. In addition to providing the land, they participated in and oversaw the construction and now manage its maintenance and operation. They know every inch of it and the meaning and significance of the myriad treasures it contains.

Their Buddhist practice is central to their identities, but they also have other creative interests. Stan plays guitar and sings folk music and was once in a rock group. He created whimsical works of folk art, and Shirley constructed wooden boxes inlaid with intricate patterns carved from exotic wood. Although Stan still performs folk music on occasion, their other arts no longer have significant roles in their lives. Now they express most of their creativity through the stupa and the events that take place there.

Our first trip to the stupa occurred because we had bumped into

Stan and Shirley a few days earlier at El Morro National Monument, and they had invited us to come out for a visit. Bhakha Tulku, the revered rinpoche under whose auspices the stupa exists, was with them at the monument, and I greeted him and shook his hand. The man's energy was palpable—our brief encounter left me charged with energy.

Stan told me later that my contact with the rinpoche was great luck. Bhakha Tulku had just completed a visit to Bhutan, where he was ceremoniously carried off the plane and celebrated for days. Hundreds of people had walked for many miles just to catch a glimpse of him, and I had gone right up to him and shook his hand.

We first heard about the Zuni Mountain Stupa at a potluck supper that Stan and Shirley held for a few neighbors and friends to introduce their plans before construction began in 2004. In attendance was a rinpoche from California who had taken on the task of aiding in the stupa planning and building and making sure that the exact strictures for its proper construction were met. He was Tibetan and his open and engaging manner quickly connected him with everyone.

We filled our plates, sat down under the trees, and listened to talks about the stupa and the coming building process. During a lull in the presentations an old white-haired guy, one of the neighbors, smiled and said, "I guess a little spirituality never hurt anyone." For some reason, the rinpoche and I both found this hilarious and heart-warming, and we started laughing. The man's comment was a casual expression of acceptance, a reaching across the spiritual and cultural divide between himself and the Tibetan priest. It was one of those moments we tend to remember, when people who don't really know each other move together in a kindred way.

The consecration and celebration of the completed stupa occurred in September 2009. It was a fine day, an exotic combination of color, music, ceremony, and dance. Many Tibetan Buddhists attended, mixed in with other visitors and locals. There were Tibetan dances, a procession of rinpoches in full regalia, and food, fires, gongs, drums, and horns, all flowing around the new stupa and the wide meadow it graced.

Even though heavy afternoon storms swirled around the site, only a few clouds and sprinkles dampened the meadow. We feared stormy weather on the way home, however, so we left in the late afternoon. Our drive took us through flooded areas and pouring rain, but we made it safely to our house.

Others, especially those who lingered longer before leaving, were not so lucky. Cars got washed into ditches and stuck in the mud and some areas became inaccessible because of high water. Shortly after our arrival home the road into our area became completely impassable when Highway 53 was flooded with a roiling, five-foot-deep flow of stormwater and mud. Many could not make it back until the next day.

When we went out the following morning we saw that parts of the land on either side of our highway turnoff were much higher than usual. Apparently, despite the relative warmth of those September days, what appeared to be some three feet of sediment was really made up of hailstones with a thin topping of pine needles and soil. The hail had fallen higher up the canyon, washed down, and deposited below. By the next day the hail had all melted and the topography returned to what it was before the storm.

The Zuni Mountain Stupa is one of several stupas in New Mexico, mostly located along the valley of the Rio Grande River north of Albuquerque. Some, like the Zuni Mountain Stupa, are fairly large, and others are much smaller. We were familiar, for instance, with a small stupa that had once been on Petroglyph National Monument land, a very short distance from where we live now.

Before Congress authorized the creation of the Petroglyph National Monument in 1990, Harold Cohen and his wife owned the land on which it stands. Harold was a psychiatrist, and both were friends of Bear Heart and Reginah. Their stupa had been built properly in the traditional manner, filled with Tibetan Buddhist relics and hundreds of pages of mantra texts and consecrated by a

Tibetan lama. Although, including its spire, it stood only ten feet tall and was made of solid concrete without an interior space, it had all the spiritual significance of any other stupa.

Once the Petroglyph National Monument was established, the law required that the small stupa be relocated. It was eventually removed by John Ojile, a local Tibetan Buddhist lama, who placed it on his land in the Tijeras Canyon on the eastern side of Albuquerque, where it now overlooks Interstate 40. A Buddhist belief holds that just seeing a stupa gives blessings, so I-40 travelers who catch a passing glimpse of it may notice that they suddenly feel a little better.

Back when Harold still owned the land he invited Bear Heart to set up a teepee near the stupa. Reginah told us that on some mornings Bear Heart would sit at the opening of the teepee facing the stupa and chant, while Harold sat at the front of the stupa facing the teepee and played a flute, the men greeting each other and the morning in their own ways. I like the image of those two expressing their mutual affection and respect for each other's spiritual and cultural traditions. I also like the fact that in both their beliefs no religion is superior to another.

One day, when Matt and his family were visiting, we decided to show them the Zuni Mountain Stupa. We thought this would be of particular interest to Matt's wife, Eed, who is Buddhist, and on our way we stopped at the Ancient Way Café on Highway 53 in El Morroville for lunch. In addition to being a very good restaurant, the Ancient Way Café is a high spot of diversity and creativity.

The café is owned by Sharron, a retired Texas prison warden, and two of its denizens are Standing Feather, an artist and proprietor of an eclectic art gallery, and his partner, RedWulf, who has been everything from circus clown to Reiki practitioner. Like many people in the area, they are both excellent poets. They live at the Ancient Way Café, are involved in the operation of the restaurant and the rental cabins, and also provide tarot readings and shamanic vision journeys.

When we arrived at the restaurant we were surprised to see Standing Feather, RedWulf, and a couple of other people setting up a stage in front of the restaurant porch. Maqui, another Ancient Way denizen and a fine potter, would give an outdoor performance that night featuring his popular channeling of Janis Joplin. We greeted everyone, went inside, squeezed around a table, and ordered.

While we waited for our food, Melani, a doctor at the Zuni Public Health Service Indian Hospital and Sharron's partner, came in. Although we didn't know it at the time, Melani speaks passable Thai because of a stint with the Peace Corps in Thailand. We introduced her to our family and before long I heard Melani, Matt, and Eed chattering away in Thai.

After our food came and we settled down to eat, a group on motorcycles roared up and walked in. They began speaking in Spanish and Sharron, who was at the desk, asked if anyone in the restaurant could help with translation. I speak a bit of Spanish, so I volunteered, and it turned out that the motorcyclists were all from Barcelona, Spain, on a cross-country tour, and they needed directions.

Finally, on the way out we met a man who was setting up a movie camera. He had heard about the Ramah area and its rich diversity and wanted to portray it cinematically. Imagine that: stopping in a rural New Mexico restaurant for lunch and having all these experiences, with the stellar stupa yet to come.

34. Exploder

WHEN YOU LIVE IN a place like Timberlake Ranch a two-wheel-drive sedan is probably not the best car to have. Many of the roads are dirt and gravel and they may be rough, snow-covered, or deep in mud. You need something sturdy. Four-wheel drive is a good idea, but higher clearance for ruts and snow might be even more important.

That's why, just before we moved to New Mexico in 1997, we bought a Ford Explorer. It was comfortable and functional, and we called it the Green Machine. I used it to haul stones I found here and there for building walks and flower beds. It carried us on trips and through tilted and eroded roads that we never thought we could navigate. We put 130,000 miles on it over eighteen years or so, and it was a good and dependable friend.

Jody, our mechanic in Ramah, fixed it time and again, and tried to help us with costs by getting parts for it from another old Explorer he had in his yard. Because our roads had so many nails scattered on them, he patched flat tire after flat tire. I had a jar where I put nails and screws and a few other things pulled from our tires, and it held dozens of them by the time we moved. Eventually, the flat tire problem eased when Jody rigged up a magnetic bar that hung down in front of the road grader and picked up most of the nails on the roads in Timberlake.

One winter night we went to an event at the Old School Gallery with two friends, George and Nancy, and as we drove home in the Green Machine through snow and dark on Highway 53, our headlights went out. Suddenly, we were swinging through tree-lined curves on a slippery road and all we could see through the windshield was pitch black.

I frantically pumped the brakes and pushed this and that, but the lights didn't come back on until I pulled back on the headlight dimmer handle. We all heaved a sigh of relief when I discovered the lights would continue to shine as long as I kept pressure on the handle. George and Nancy later decided it all was a hoot; they were sure I had done it as a joke.

The next day the headlights worked fine, so we didn't worry about them until a few weeks later, when it happened again. We took the car to Jody, who, despite trying everything he could think of, couldn't fix the problem. Even though he kept the car for a week, put in a new dimmer switch, and tested it under various conditions, he couldn't make it recur so he could trace the cause. After that we only drove it during the day and, even then, not often, because, in addition to the headlight problem, the left front door had gotten to where it wouldn't open without a very hard yank. That was about when we stopped calling the car the Green Machine and began jokingly referring to it as the Exploder.

Because of the risk posed by the headlight problem, we knew we couldn't sell or give the car away, so we decided that we would eventually donate it to Jody for parts. We liked the symbolism; the parts he had scavenged for the car would return to the source to be used as needed for other failing Explorers that limped into his garage. It would be a kind of full-circle mechanical organ donation.

One day our friend Maryanna was going to drop by for a visit, but because of the condition of our roads and her car's low clearance, I picked her up in the Exploder at the Ancient Way Café and drove her to our house. After our visit she and I headed back toward the café on Highway 53 so she could pick up her car. We had only gone a few miles when we noticed wisps of smoke coming from the vent in front of the windshield. I pulled over, opened the front hood, and discovered a mouse nest of leaves and pine needles smoldering among the wiring. I pulled it out, closed the lid, and asked Maryanna to stand in front and watch the car as I tried to start it again.

The Exploder started and I thought we could go on our way, but Maryanna yelled and pointed at smoke that was again leaking from the vent. When I jumped out and opened the hood again, flames engulfed the engine. I slammed the hood in hopes that the fire would go out, but when we spotted flames flickering more brightly in the vent and around the windshield, we called 911.

Fire trucks from two volunteer fire departments and Zuni police officers arrived on the scene, but in the short time it took them to get there the car had become totally enveloped in flames. The firefighters tried hosing it down, but the car quickly burned to a charred, black metal frame.

When given the bare facts it sounds like a sad and harrowing experience, but for me it wasn't. Many of the people who responded, especially the firefighters, were sympathetic friends and neighbors, and their presence was a comfort and a safety measure against the possibility that it could start a grass fire. We were about to give the car to Jody for parts, a somewhat ignoble ending for what I thought of as a noble beast. Instead I got to watch as it burned gloriously beside the road, kind of like a Viking warrior's funeral barge. It was a great send-off.

When Jody came out and winched it up on his truck, I stuck my head in his window. "This was your car?" he said with surprise.

"Yes," I responded. "We were about to give it to you for parts." Despite luckily not exploding, it lived up to the spirit of its name by going out in a great conflagration.

This situation is not unusual for the area; a mouse will make a nest on the engine of a car and it will catch fire. Some people check under their hoods regularly for nests, especially if their car is parked outside and not driven often.

The Exploder had been our companion for almost all our time living in the area; shortly after it burned, we moved to Albuquerque. We later heard that another Ford Explorer had done the same thing on Highway 53 within a mile or so of our burn site. In that case, the fire occurred while the car was still on the tarmac. It melted the tar and got stuck, and it cost four hundred dollars to remove it from the road's surface. We heard the owner couldn't afford the expense, so the car sat there for weeks, surrounded by hazard tape like some kind of weird art installation. But we knew it was just the remains of another Exploder cremation awaiting its final disposition.

35. Duke City

ON A SNOWY JANUARY afternoon in 2018, we drove away from our Ramah area home for the last time. After slogging through muddy roads to Highway 53, we turned toward Grants, New Mexico, and the title company. Sale papers were signed, keys were delivered, and on we went toward Albuquerque and the next chapter in our lives. As we approached the city in the early evening on I-40, the sky cleared. We crested the hill above Albuquerque and saw the Sandia Mountains glowing crimson in the setting sun and the city lights glittering like crystals along the Rio Grande.

We were sad to leave the place and the people we loved, but we were in our seventies and needed to move on to an easier lifestyle. Lucia's son Tim and his family lived in Albuquerque, as did my cousin Edgar and his family, our niece Oakley, and several friends, including some who'd moved there from the Ramah area. We weren't going far; we told friends that we were only moving to the El Morroville suburbs, 140 miles down the road.

I had a long familiarity with Albuquerque. In the 1950s I occasionally went there in the summer to spend a week or two with Uncle Ed, Aunt Martha, and their two kids, Edgar and Martha. My parents would buy me a ticket and put me on a TWA Constellation airplane at the Wichita airport, and Uncle Ed's family would greet me on the other end of the flight.

Because we boys were close in age, Edgar was my main pal. Albuquerque was a much smaller city then, about a hundred thousand people, compared to its metropolitan population approaching a million today. I remember wandering around a pueblo ruin on the edge of town, a foreshadowing of experiences that awaited me decades later.

Lucia and I occasionally visited Albuquerque during our early years together, mostly when we were building our house in Timberlake. In 1990 we stayed a couple of nights in the first bed and breakfast established in Albuquerque, Casita Chamisa, located in the pastoral North Valley. It was an old, restored adobe, and a fascinating archaeological dig lay beneath it.

After breakfast the first morning, our hosts, the Sargeants, led us down a staircase in the kitchen to the basement, where a dirt wall was marked with dates going back hundreds of years. Mrs. Sargeant was an archeologist, and she pointed out areas in the wall where we could see ashes from ancient cooking fires and other indications of human presence.

We could almost feel the multitude of peoples who had inhabited the spot where the house stood, drawn there by the water, game, and timber along the Rio Grande. Eventually, the Sargeants financed and managed another archaeological dig beside their house that uncovered ruins of an adobe village and evidence of six other temporal layers of occupation, the oldest around the year 1300.

The earliest human habitation in the Albuquerque area goes back as far as twelve thousand years, when people there may have hunted mastodons. Then came waves of others: Ancestral Puebloans, Pueblo Indians, nomadic tribes, and everyone else. The city of Albuquerque itself is well over three hundred years old, founded in 1706 as a Spanish colonial outpost on the Camino Real, the Spanish road into the interior lands of their settlements. It was named in honor of the tenth duke of Albuquerque who was viceroy over the entire Spanish territory in this hemisphere. In April 1862 it was the site of a battle during the Civil War.

The Rio Grande flows through the heart of the city. On the east side of the river Albuquerque rises into the foothills of the Sandia Mountains, and on the west side it extends out of the valley and over a long line of bluffs. Our house is on the western bluffs, a couple of miles from the Petroglyph National Monument.

The Petroglyph Monument is named after the figures and patterns carved into large stones by Ancestral Pueblo people and early Spanish settlers. There are some twenty-four thousand images there, going back as far as three thousand years. It is also where, before the monument was established, our friend Bear Heart sat in a teepee and chanted to his friend, Harold Cohen, who sat facing him in front of his Buddhist stupa.

As anywhere, Albuquerque has its own mix of life forms that give it character and connect us to the natural world. We've seen coyotes skirting our house and running down the street, a Cooper's hawk we named Slim who waits patiently in a tree above our bird feeder to take an occasional pigeon, and cottontail rabbits that graze on our tiny lawn. But for us the three natural totems here are cottonwood trees, sandhill cranes, and roadrunners.

I remember from my Kansas childhood the cottonwood trees that bordered a small lake where we fished for bass, bluegills, and crappies. The largest trees were strung along the dam of the lake, and they were a welcome comfort when we sat below them at night, fishing for channel catfish. They were a frustration, though, in the late spring, because their seeds were attached to fluffs of white that resembled cotton. The cotton floated on the lake surface, sometimes so thickly that it had to be painstakingly stripped from our fishing lines after every cast.

In Albuquerque cottonwoods are the primary trees in the bosque (riparian woodland) that runs along the Rio Grande and in other places abundant with soil water. Their cotton floats through the air in late May and June, and some areas beneath the trees appear blanketed in snow. In autumn their leaves turn bright yellow, creating wide, golden swaths where the river flows through the city. In winter stark cottonwood branches trace sinuous patterns against the blue New Mexico sky.

November brings sandhill cranes by the thousands to Albuquerque, and some remain throughout the winter. They are majestic birds, standing over four feet tall with long legs and necks, and their voices can carry for two and a half miles. I was walking one day across a mall parking lot during our first year here, listening to their distinctive cry but unable to see them. I finally spotted them overhead, flying in their characteristic V formation, so high that they were barely visible.

When November rolls around we usually yearn for a concentrated crane fix, so we drive one hundred miles south of Albuquerque to the Bosque del Apache National Wildlife Refuge, where dozens of wetlands have been restored in the Rio Grande floodplain. There, along with some fifty thousand snow geese and other waterfowl, around fifteen thousand sandhill cranes spend the winter.

The wildlife refuge was established in 1939 by President Franklin Roosevelt, and it extends over fifty-seven thousand acres. It contains a series of roads that wind around wetlands and fields where corn and triticale (a hybrid of wheat and rye) are planted as food for the birds. Watching flocks of sandhills return in the evening is really something; they curve their great wings to reduce their speed, lower their long legs, flare at the last moment, and drop gently into the shallow water.

Finally, the roadrunner is one of the most engaging and fascinating of birds, even more impressive in real life than in its cartoon representations. They are fairly large—up to twenty-four inches in length—slender, white-streaked birds with long, cocked tails and distinctive head crests. You can usually see them standing or darting across the ground, and they can run up to twenty miles an hour. Fearless and cocky, they eat many of the scary beasts written about in this book, including rattlesnakes and tarantulas, and they are the only predator with enough hutzpah to gobble down tarantula hawk wasps.

The Ramah area had some roadrunners, but they seem more present in Albuquerque, where they are surprisingly comfortable in the urban setting. We have spotted them in a Costco parking lot, looking in the window of a Thai restaurant, on the front porch of our friend Susan's house waiting for a handout, and in our own front yard. We named our resident roadrunner Roadie. Susan named hers Rudy, and he often accompanied her on walks.

Tim and his family moved from Alaska to Albuquerque, and he has fallen under the area's spell. He goes to the Ramah area as often as he can, to his own piece of land that overlooks the lake, and talks about moving there one day. He once told me that he occasionally missed the green of Alaska. I asked him, "Do you wish you hadn't moved?"

"No," he said. "I love it here. I just sometimes miss the green."

We feel the same way about our home, Cielo. Of course, we miss being there sometimes. We miss our friends, the natural beauty, the stars, and the spirit of the place. I became so accustomed to hugging almost everyone there that I still occasionally forget and press a hug on an unwilling Albuquerque acquaintance. But missing our home in Timberlake does not diminish the contentment we have here in Albuquerque.

36. Talking Pots

I AM A SCAVENGER by nature and have been since I was a little boy. Whenever I am on a walk I continuously search for treasures. They might be a deer skull, an unusual stone, or a strangely twisted branch. When I come across them I feel a rush of happiness. As a young boy I often walked the red hills outside the town of Medicine Lodge, Kansas, looking for arrowheads. I could imagine braves on horseback on top of the bluffs, and I just knew they must have once been there and left arrowheads behind, but I never found one.

When I got to our new home in the Ramah area, the scavenger in me was in heaven. In addition to all the natural treasures, there were artifacts left behind by the Ancient Puebloans, especially pottery sherds. But those things are best left where they are.

It is illegal, in fact, to remove artifacts, including sherds, from federal, New Mexico, or tribal lands, or to disturb burial sites anywhere. Also, legality aside, artifacts should remain in place to preserve their archeological value, and so the next person who passes by can appreciate them. And, odd as it may sound, that's where the artifacts want to be.

In October 2019 I came across an article in *New Mexico Magazine* about the return of pots created by the Tewa people to the Poeh

Cultural Center Museum in Pojoaque. Pojoaque is one of six Tewa pueblos located along or near the Rio Grande north of Santa Fe. The pots had been collected from the tribes by anthropologists during the late 1800s and early 1900s and brought to the Smithsonian National Museum of the American Indian. Representatives of all six of the Tewa pueblos spent two years selecting the one hundred items that would be returned to their New Mexico place of origin.

This sounds like a normal process for transferring items between museums, which it was until the Indigenous belief that there is spirit in everything manifested itself. During the two years of the pot selection process, the Tewa representatives talked with the pots. They had a series of conversations with them "to remind them of their language, and thereby prepare them for the journey home."

Shortly after reading the article we drove over one afternoon to visit the talking pots. As we entered the museum we were greeted by a friendly young Pojoaque man. He gave us a tour and told us how honored he was to accompany the elders on a couple of their trips to select the pots, which to them are living extensions of their families and communities.

The pots are, indeed, extraordinary. From very large to very small, there are pitchers, dough bowls, and shapes of people, animals, and kivas. They are black and white, brown and white, and polychrome, and decorated with traditional and creative patterns. And the way the Tewa people revere them and returned them to their home is a good model for humanity, as we try to help the fragile blue marble of our earth return to a state of stability and health.

It is equally important, though, that we heal our relationships with each other; shift our lives and nations to recognize that we are a global community. People are communal by nature, which is useful for maintaining identity and culture, but in today's interconnected world it places us all in peril when community becomes a way to justify dominating and exploiting outsiders.

This doesn't mean we somehow become one great kumbaya harmonic chorus; there will always be places and times of stress and conflict and inequality. People and countries will have differing opinions on paths to take, and that is how we learn and grow.

If, however, we develop a fundamental commitment to the rights that all have in common, we will have a much better chance to survive. And this must go beyond lip service. Our commitment to each other will only hold if nations acknowledge and work together to implement and enforce the reality that the world is socially, economically, electronically, and environmentally interdependent. Clinging to the concept that any country today has absolute sovereignty is a path to disaster.

One of the first things I learned as a lawyer with Indian law responsibilities was that Native tribes in this country are, by federal law, "domestic dependent nations," a strange but accurate concept; tribes are both sovereign and dependent. There is some irony in the fact that this country, which has historically wrested so much sovereignty from its Native people, must now yield some of its own sovereignty to function effectively in the context of the interdependent world.

Can we do it? During my last few years at EPA we held quarterly public meetings in each of our four states, Kansas, Missouri, Iowa, and Nebraska, to listen to environmental concerns. At one of those meetings a woman came up to me afterward and told me that global warming had already progressed beyond the point of no return. In her opinion it didn't matter what we did; we were already doomed. I asked her gently, "If that's the case, why did you come to this meeting?" She was taken aback and didn't have an answer.

But I know why. An old friend of mine, Wes Jackson, founder of the Land Institute in Manhattan, Kansas, and a leading light of the sustainable agricultural movement, once said, "I'm an intellectual pessimist but a glandular optimist." That describes the woman at the meeting, and it is how I identify too. The intellectual pessimists in both of us say the challenges are overwhelming, but our glandular optimists beg to differ.

There are glimmers of hope. Nations are beginning to move more widely together on shared challenges of pandemics, transnational aggression, and global warming. And communities like the one we inhabited in New Mexico exist, where strangers are offered hugs instead of handshakes, and the energy of the natural world is transcendent.

In our common ancestral heritage we humans are all indigenous to the earth, sisters and brothers of the same tribe, and through our molecular heritage, children together of the stars. The hippies got at least one thing right: we really are stardust, and somehow, I believe, we will make our way back to the garden.

Further Reading

Below please find a list of titles mentioned in the text, in the order in which they appear:

Baling Wire and Gamuza, Barbara Vogt Mallery (*New Mexico Magazine*, 2003).

> An intimate memoir in text and photography of life from 1905 to 1986 on a family ranch near Ramah, New Mexico.

Sallie Fox: The Story of a Pioneer Girl, Dorothy Kupcha Leland (Tomato Enterprises, 1995).

> A popular and true story of a pioneer girl who, with her family, traveled in a wagon from Iowa to California. Along the way she inscribed her name and the year, 1858, on the cliff at El Morro National Monument.

First Impressions: A Reader's Journey to Iconic Places of the American Southwest, David J. Weber and William deBuys (Yale University Press, 2017).

> Through the words of early non-Native explorers and their own impressions, two celebrated historians take the reader on a fascinating journey of mystery and discovery through fifteen iconic Southwestern sites.

An American Sunrise, Joy Harjo (W. W. Norton and Company, 2019).

> A volume of narrative and poetry addressing the author's personal and tribal history. Joy Harjo, a member of the Muscogee Creek Nation, is a celebrated poet and former United States Poet Laurate.

House Made of Dawn, N. Scott Momaday (HarperCollins, 1934).
A Pulitzer Prize–winning novel about the difficulties
encountered by a Native man born in New Mexico who is
pulled by the two disparate worlds of tribal and dominant
culture. N. Scott Momaday, a member of the Kiowa Nation,
is a celebrated novelist, poet, and artist.

The Overview Effect, Frank White (Houghton Mifflin, 1987).
An exploration of the powerful mental and emotional shift
toward protecting the earth that occurs when our planet is
observed from space.

West of the Thirties: Discoveries Among the Navajo and Hopi, Edward
T. Hall (Anchor Books, 1995).
The experiences and insights of anthropologist Edward
T. Hall as he lived and worked from 1933 to 1937 in the
Southwest, where four cultures—Navajo, Hopi, Hispanic,
and Anglo—intersect.

Anam Cara, John O'Donohue (HarperCollins, 1997).
A treasure of philosophic reflection, based in Irish/Celtic
tradition.

Esteban, Dennis Harrick (University of New Mexico Press, 2018).
The life of Esteban is central to the history of the American
Southwest, and Herrick's gift as a storyteller and his subtle
reflections make this a highly interesting and engaging
read.

The Genízaro and the Artist, Napoleon Garcia (Rio Grande Books, 2008).
A recounting of the Genízaro author's life on the Abiquiú,
New Mexico, Spanish land grant made to his ancestors
in 1754 and his relationship with his employer, the artist
Georgia O'Keeffe.

The Mexican Frontier, 1821–1846, David J. Weber (University of
New Mexico Press, 1982).
A history of the short period of Mexican rule over the
American Southwest, by the preeminent historian of the

Spanish empire in North America. David and his wife, Carol, were our neighbors and friends in the Ramah area.

Memories of Cibola, Abe Peña (University of New Mexico Press, 1997).

An engaging and folksy description of the author's early years growing up in the small Hispanic village of San Mateo, New Mexico.

En Divina Luz, Craig Varjabedian and Michael Wallis (University of New Mexico Press, 1994).

A beautiful volume of text and photography detailing Penitente moradas (churches) in New Mexico.

The Milagro Beanfield War, John Nichols (Holt, Reinhart, and Winston, 1974).

A novel about a water war that begins in a tiny New Mexico bean field. The first installment of Nichols's acclaimed New Mexico trilogy.

The Wind Is My Mother: The Life and Teachings of a Native American Shaman, Bear Heart with Molly Larkin (Clarkson N. Potter, 1996).

A blending of the personal story and teachings of a widely revered Muscogee Creek medicine man who was also a roadman in the Native American Church and a Baptist minister.

The Bear Is My Father, Marcellus "Bear Heart" Williams and Reginah WaterSpirit (Synergetic Press, 2021).

A companion to *The Wind Is My Mother*, with additional Bear Heart reflections and teachings. Threaded throughout is the autobiographical story of his medicine helper and late-life spouse.

Quanah Parker, Comanche Chief, William T. Hagan (University of Oklahoma Press, 1993).

A biography of the Cherokee/white man who created the Native American Church and later served as an effective champion on pivotal Native rights issues.

Building the Zuni Mountain Stupa, Shirley Giser (self-published, 2019).
The detailed story, with color photos, of the construction
of the Zuni Mountain Stupa, including the spiritual
significance of the stupa's entirety and many of its elements.

Talking with the Clay: The Art of Pueblo Pottery in the 21st Century,
Stephen Trimble (School for Advanced Research Press, 2007).
A moving collection of text and photos that illuminates the
pottery and potters of a number of New Mexico pueblos,
with particular focus on the long tradition and spiritual
nature of this ancient art form.